When
FOOTBALL *Was*
FOOTBALL

MANCHESTER
CITY

First published in 2010

A catalogue record for this book is available from the British Library

ISBN: 978-0-857330-37-6

Published by Haynes Publishing, Sparkford, Yeovil,
Somerset BA22 7JJ, UK
Tel: 01963 442030 Fax: 01963 440001
Int. tel: +44 1963 442030 Int. fax: +44 1963 440001
E-mail: sales@haynes.co.uk
Website: www.haynes.co.uk

Haynes North America Inc., 861 Lawrence Drive,
Newbury Park, California 91320, USA

All images © Mirrorpix

Creative Director: Kevin Gardner
Designed for Haynes by BrainWave

Printed and bound in the US

When
FOOTBALL *Was*
FOOTBALL

MANCHESTER CITY

A Nostalgic Look at a Century of the Club

David Clayton

Contents

Foreword

We've got no history, apparently...

I know this because I've heard opposing fans sing it. I know this because I've heard pundits say it. I know this thanks to Javier Mascherano, who earlier this year declared: "I don't want to play for Manchester City. You can buy players, but you cannot buy history. At Liverpool, we play with the history of the club."*

The cure for this ignorance? A copy of this book, preferably delivered with force to the back of the head. This will hurt, of course, but then there's rather a lot of history inside: Bert's neck, the Revie Plan, Buzzer, Franny and Young; Gornik Zabrze, Gillingham; Anna Connell; Horace Barnes, Ken Barnes and Peter Barnes; Alan Oakes and Paul Power; Joe and Big Mal, and Colin the King.

This is our history, and we're proud of every bit of it. The wider point, of course, is that all clubs can and must say the same. History isn't the preserve of those who are winning now, or those who won in the recent past. It's Raddy Bloody Antic, Ricky Bloody Villa and Alan Ball's missing radio; Mike Summerbee and the fast, fast and more fast David White; Bolton April 1904, St James' Park May 1968, Maine Road September 23, 1989; Tommy Johnson, Eric Brook and Peter Doherty; Dennis Tueart's overhead, Steve Mackenzie's volley and Hutch's goal at either end; Hyde Road, the Windy Corner, Gene Kelly Stand and the scoreboard that never worked.

As Henry Ford nearly said, "you've got no history" is bunk.

Steve Anglesey, summer 2010

*Given our new circumstances, there's always the chance that Mascherano might actually be playing for City by the time you read this. In which case, welcome to Manchester, Javier. Always liked you.

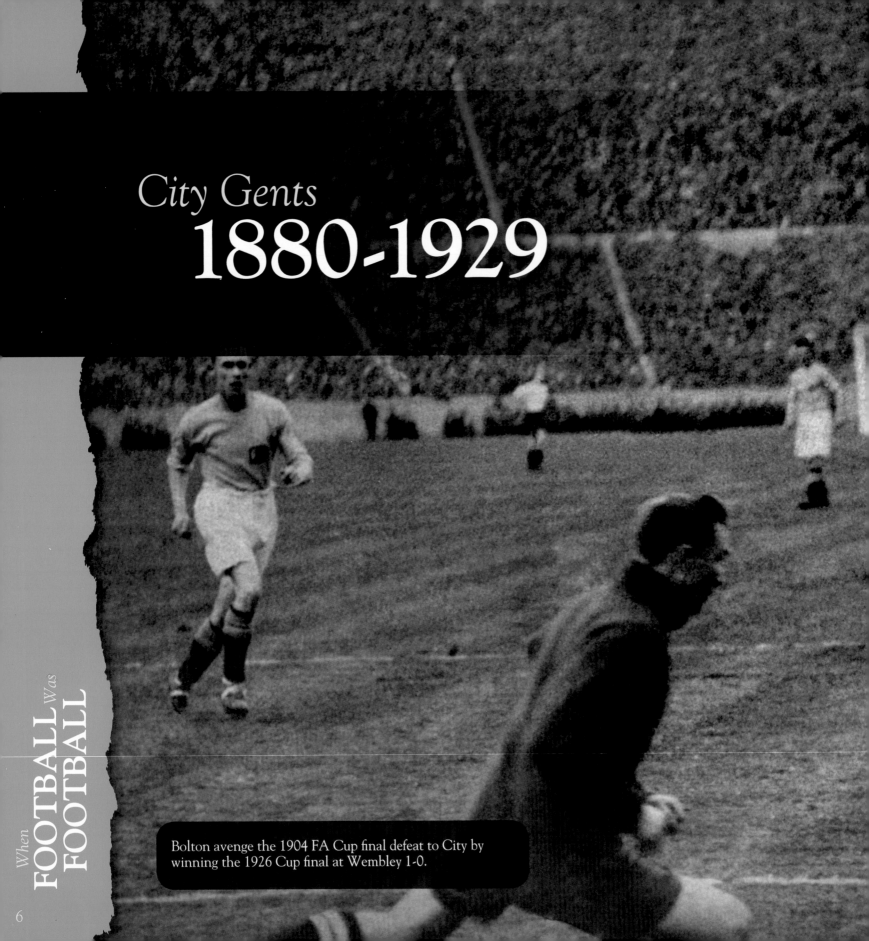

Bolton avenge the 1904 FA Cup final defeat to City by winning the 1926 Cup final at Wembley 1-0.

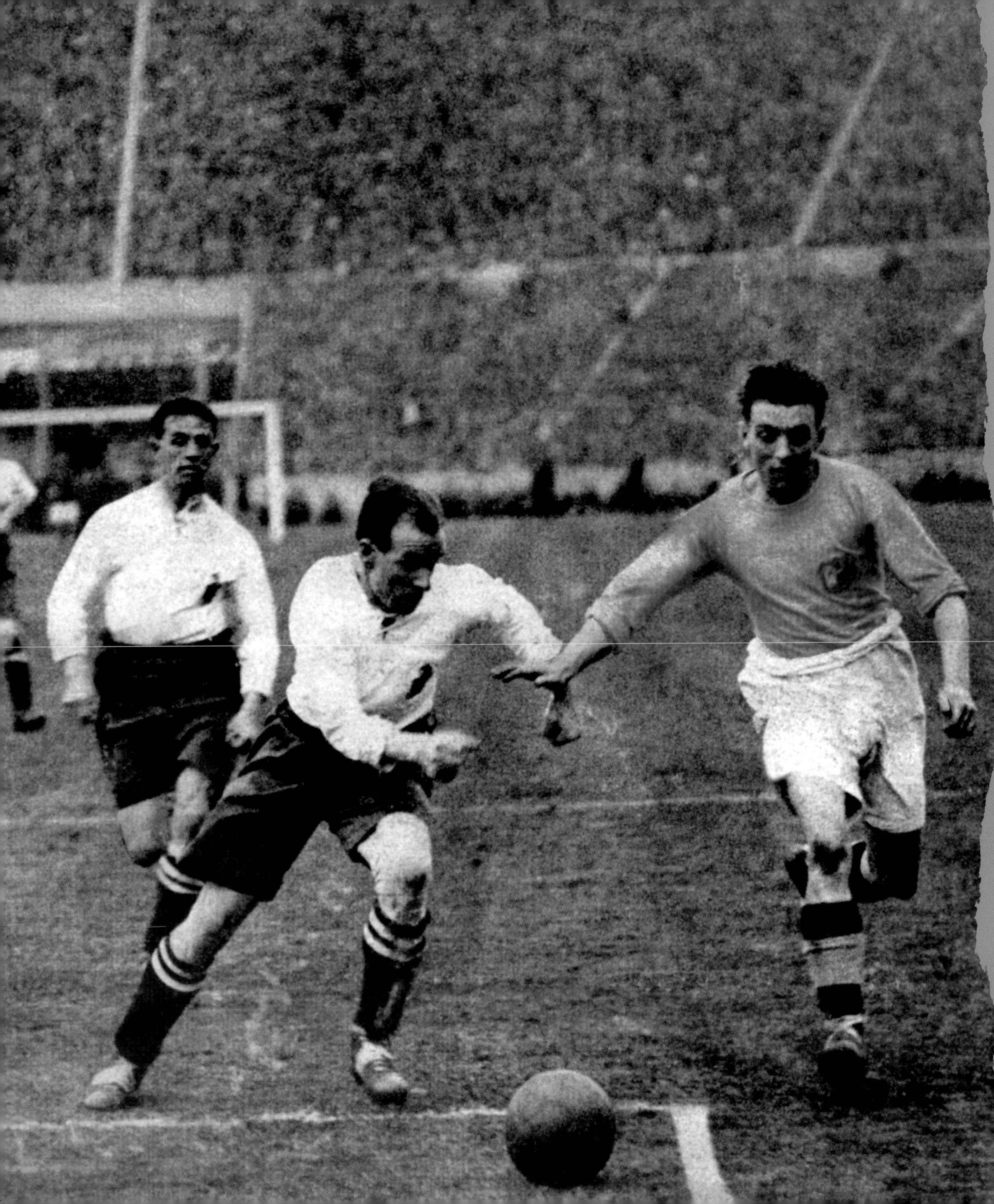

1880 St Mark's (West Gorton) formed by Anna Connell and two churchwardens and play home games at various locations around East Manchester. 1887 Club move to Hyde Road and rename as Ardwick FC. 1892 Ardwick join the Football League Second Division, but struggle financially, and during the 1893/4 campaign the club re-emerge as Manchester City FC. 1899 City win Second Division – the club's first silverware – and take their place in the top division for the first time. 1902 City are relegated for the first time. 1903 City win Division Two for second time. 1904 City win the FA Cup after beating Bolton Wanderers 1-0 at The Crystal Palace and narrowly miss out on an historic League and Cup double after finishing second to champions The Wednesday. 1905 The club suspend 17 players, including the talismanic Billy Meredith, on suspicion of financial irregularities – many join Manchester United who reap the rewards. 1909 City are relegated. 1910 City win Division Two for third time in 11 years. 1915 The First World War halts the Football League for four years. 1920 The Main Stand at Hyde Road is destroyed in a fire, prompting a move to Moss Side and a new stadium designed by renowned architect Charles Swain. 1921 City finish runners-up in Division One. 1923 City play their final match at Hyde Road. Maine Road opens its gates for the first time as City beat Sheffield United 2-1. 1926 City take on Bolton at Wembley in a repeat of the 1904 final – but Bolton are the 1-0 victors this time. City are relegated days after losing the Cup final. 1928 City win Division Two for the fourth time.

APRIL 25, 1904.

MANCHESTER WIN "T' COOP."

Bolton Were Cheered by Southern Football Enthusiasts, but Without Avail.

MEREDITH'S GREAT GOAL.

The Manchester City Club won the Football Association Cup from the Bolton Wanderers at the Crystal Palace on Saturday afternoon by 1 goal to nil. The national football trophy thus finds an entirely new resting place for a season. It has been to Blackburn—which is quite adjacent—often, but never to Manchester.

According to the official estimates, over 61,000 persons witnessed the play. This was by no means a big gate, considering that the clubs in opposition were near neighbours hailing from the same county. At least two-thirds of the spectators were partizans of one or other of the teams, for the railway companies confess that they ran nearly sixty specials from the North, carrying altogether about 40,000 people to town. It is thus seen that London generally was not greatly interested in the function, although every Metropolitan footballer of note who could spare the time was present at the match.

There has never been a Final Tie at the Palace which has not been favoured with fine weather. Saturday was no exception to the rule. It was a glorious afternoon—warm and sunny—with here and there a short spell of cloudiness and a trifling threat of rain. The conditions could not have been improved, for the ground, in spite of the deluge overnight, was beautifully green and elastic, while there was little or no wind. It only remained for the two elevens to play at the very top of their form in order that we might witness a struggle in every way worthy of the importance of the occasion.

Bolton the Favourites.

Shrewd sportsmen selected Manchester City the probable winners, but once the men had entered the field of play one could make no mistake as to which side had caught the popular fancy. Whatever Bolton did that was hopeful of fruit or clever in execution was cheered to the echo. The applause that fell to the lot of Manchester City was neither so strong in volume nor so frequent. The Cockney element in the crowd showed its sympathy for the supposed-to-be weaker side in characteristically sporting fashion. The verdict of the northern partizans at the close was "hard lines."

Bolton took their defeat very quietly. Several of their travel-stained and footsore supporters were not in such an equable frame of mind. There were several very spirited battles of words on the grassy slopes just after the match, although no blows were struck. The Manchester men were inclined to "crow" over their victory, and naturally the Wanderers' followers felt resentful. By midnight, however, all differences had been arranged, and the two factions returned to their native Lancashire friendly, but, in many cases, not a little fuddled. This was not accomplished, however, until Fleet-street, the Strand, and the West End generally had been made to ring with their ear-splitting football slogans. It was a great day for Lancashire in general, and Manchester in particular.

A description of the play would be out of place here, for every incident has been chronicled a thousand times over since Saturday evening. It was not a great match by any means—very few finals are—but it was one of the hardest and most determined ever seen on the ground. The men were overwhelmed with anxiety to play their very best, and, as a consequence, each side fell far short of its own expectations, as well as those of its supporters. The boast about the brilliant dribbling and short passing qualities of the Manchester men was not borne out by the play. There were here and there glimpses of that mechanical combination which is so delightful to the eye of the old player, but each scientific effort seemed to break down at the point where it seemed most likely to lead to tangible results.

Bolton were evidently not consumed with anxiety to distinguish themselves as professors of the art of football finesse. They had their objective, and they made for it with such heartiness and vigour that it was little wonder that they were by far the more popular team before the struggle was over. They always appeared to have a chance of winning, and it can truthfully be said that accident alone prevented them from at least drawing level on several occasions. On Saturday's showing they are not a great team—on the same basis of argument neither are Manchester City—but they were always full of fight, and they had not lost the game until it was over.

MANCHESTER CITY v. WOOLWICH.

Manchester City v. Woolwich Arsenal, at Manchester : A fine bit of head-work by a Manchester forward in the game which Manchester won by a goal to nil.

LEFT: One of the earliest *Daily Mirror* match reports of City following the 1-0 win over Bolton in the 1904 FA Cup final where Billy Meredith's 23rd-minute goal proves enough to bring the trophy back to Manchester.

ABOVE: The first published picture of City, who saw off Woolwich Arsenal 1-0 at Hyde Road.

The Daily Mirror reports on Manchester City

Manchester City Football Club were one of the biggest draws in English football by the time the *Daily Mirror* was up and running in late 1903. The crowds at Hyde Road regularly topped 25,000 and were on the increase, and football in general was booming. City had a succession of great players and their profile went through the roof after winning the FA Cup in 1904 and finishing runners-up in Division One.

MANCHESTER CITY'S OPENING PRACTICE FOR THE FOOTBALL SEASON.

Although it can hardly be realised, the football season is close at hand, and some of the leading teams are already busy practising for the coming contests. At the Hyde-road Ground at Manchester on Saturday about 8,000 spectators were present to see Manchester City's opening practice, and some good football was witnessed. (1) Smith heading out. (2) Smith saving. (3) A portion of the crowd.—(*Daily Mirror* photographs.)

LEFT: City's growing reputation ensures a spread of pre-season training pictures and evidence of the club's increasing popularity with 8,000 turning out to watch a training session at Hyde Road.

Then an FA investigation implicated star player Billy Meredith of attempting to match-fix a game against Aston Villa. The City board had suspicions of their own and refused to back Meredith when he denied the accusation, despite his importance to the team. He later admitted his role and blew the whistle on the whole scam. The result was the entire 1904 FA Cup side were effectively sacked in 1905, leaving the Blues, who had nearly completed a historic double, a broken club. With 17 players in limbo and unable to play for City again, many of them were sold at bargain prices to Manchester United. It was manna from heaven for the Reds who soon became the dominant force in the city.

FULHAM SHARE A COUPLE OF GOALS WITH MANCHESTER CITY AT CRAVEN COTTAGE.

Max Woosnam (left) and Gillespie, respective captains of Manchester City and Sheffield United, who meet in the opening match on the former club's wonderful new ground at Moss Side to-day.

Two incidents during midfield play in the Second League match between Fulham and Manchester City on Saturday. The game, which was played at Craven Cottage, resulted in a draw of 1 goal all.

ABOVE: The wording was more flowery but the information was basically the same as City draw 1-1 at Fulham.

ABOVE RIGHT INSET: Max Woosnam's photo appears prior to City's first home game at Maine Road.

FOOTBALL
–STATS–

Billy Meredith

Name: William Henry
Meredith

Born: 1874

Died: 1958

Playing career: 1890–1924

Clubs: Chirk, Northwich
Victoria, Manchester
City, Manchester United,
Manchester City

City appearances: 394

Goals: 151

—LEGENDS—

Billy Meredith
1894-05 and 1921-24

Billy Meredith may have played for City for the first time over 100 years ago, but his legend lives on to this day. Meredith – a somewhat controversial character – is ranked by many alongside the great Sir Stanley Matthews in stature and was a magnet for football fans and the media in his day. Bandy-legged and invariably chewing a toothpick, Meredith was a fantastic player and the scourge of many an Edwardian defender. The immensely talented right-winger could pinpoint a cross for a forward or cut inside and lash the ball home himself if the mood took him.

With 151 goals for the club, he is among the all-time top-scorers for City. He joined Manchester United in 1905 after the match-fixing scandal and returned to City in 1921. He also won 22 Welsh caps as a City player and holds the record for being the oldest footballer to turn out for the Blues. He was aged just 120 days short of his 50th birthday in his last game for the club – a 2-0 defeat to Newcastle United in an FA Cup semi-final. What City might have achieved had he remained with the club instead of moving on, can only be guessed.

" *Yes I smoke a pipe, but I also train twice a week, too.* "

Billy Meredith

The Wembley of the North

Just as he had done during his time with Manchester United, City boss Ernest Magnall was instrumental in City's move from the confines of Hyde Road to a new stadium in Moss Side. Ambitious plans were drawn up by architect Charles Swain to create a 120,000-capacity stadium on a patch of waste ground just off Maine Road. Magnall had played a major part in United moving from Newton Heath to Old Trafford while he was in charge of the Reds and now he was using his experience to help the Blues into a ground that was to be the finest in the country. The club had considered the Belle Vue Leisure Park, close to their original home in Ardwick, but the new site was perfect and by the beginning of the 1923/4 season, City's new home was ready for Division One football. Only the Main Stand was covered and housed seating as proud team captain Max Woosnam led the Blues out in front of a club record crowd of 56,993. It took 68 minutes for the first goal to be scored at Maine Road and the honour went to City striker Horace Barnes. The home side beat Sheffield United 2-1.

GOUGH'S INJURY.

Manchester City celebrated the opening of their new ground at Maine-road with victory over Sheffield United by the odd goal of three. Barnes and Johnson each scored in quick succession in the second half, and in stopping the second of these Gough split a finger on his right hand and had to retire.

Pantling, the one-time Watford half back, went in goal and did very well there; his successes including the saving of a penalty kick. Johnson scored the United's goal.

Everton had much the better of their game with Nottingham Forest in the first half, and scored good goals through Irvine and Hart, but after the change of ends the Foresters took a grip on the game. After Walker had scored a brilliant goal the visiting side pressed the Everton defence severely, and it was only by great good luck an equalising goal was not secured, the ball being headed away from goal no fewer than five times in the last minute of the game.

Notts County made a gratifying return to the upper division, and won a hard game with Burnley. The County scored twice a little before the interval through Hill, their inside left, but Burnley restarted with great dash and Beel reduced the lead.

> As the teams came out for the first time, the band played 'Ours is a nice house, is ours'.
>
> Manchester Evening News

ABOVE: A report on City's historic first victory in Moss Side – a 2-1 win over Sheffield United.

City's Wembley Debut

After two decades of achieving not very much, City lost the 1926 FA Cup final to Bolton Wanderers 1-0 and also their top-flight status, finishing second to bottom. David Ashworth was replaced by Peter Hodge who almost guided the club to promotion at the first attempt in 1926/7, with the Blues finishing in third place in the cruellest of circumstances. City and Portsmouth were level on points going into the final game and with both sides winning their matches, Pompey went up by the merest fraction on goal average leaving City to face another season in Division Two. In Hodge, though, they had an excellent manager and in 1927/8 the pain of the previous campaign was forgotten as the club went up as champions, averaging 38,000 at Maine Road – the highest figure anywhere in the country.

City's Jimmy McMullan and Joe Smith of Bolton shake hands before the 1926 FA Cup final, but it would be Smith who got to hold the trophy aloft after Wanderers' 1-0 victory.

15

City Slickers
1930-1949

The Duke of York shakes hands with the City players before the 1933 FA Cup final.

Peter Hodge left Maine Road in 1932 to return to one of his former clubs, Leicester City. He felt he had taken City as far as he could and Wilf Wild was promoted to manager, somewhat reluctantly. Wild's first season in charge was memorable in many ways – if not in the League where City would slump to 16th, but in the FA Cup where it was an entirely different story. Gateshead, Walsall, Bolton, Burnley and Derby were dispatched en route to Wembley to face Everton and former City hero Tommy Johnson. If that wasn't enough, the legendary Dixie Dean was also leading the line for the Merseyside giants. Everton triumphed 3-0 on the day, but City skipper Sam Cowan vowed to return the following year and lift the trophy for the Blues. Few thought it was anything other than high hopes considering the club's fortunes in the League, but Cowan was determined to make his prophecy come true.

1933 City return to Wembley but lose 3-0 to a Tommy Johnson-inspired Everton – the City fans had been dismayed when crowd favourite Johnson had been allowed to leave three years earlier after scoring 154 goals in 354 appearances during an 11-year stay. He had come back to haunt the Blues, but captain Sam Cowan promises the King that he will return the following year and win the trophy. 1934 The Blues do return to Wembley 12 months later to beat Portsmouth 2-1 in the FA Cup final – just as Cowan had predicted. 1935 Peter Doherty signs from Blackpool for a record £10,000 1937 City win First Division for the first time and do so with style and panache. 1938 Relegation for defending champions! The impossible happens when the Blues somehow go from champs to chumps within the space of a year. 1939 War breaks out and League football is suspended until 1945, meaning City effectively spend seven years outside the top flight. 1947 Sam Cowan returns to guide the Blues back to the top flight. 1948 Cowan, unwilling to move back to Manchester from his south-coast home, is forced to quit the Blues after just one season in charge.

City win the FA Cup for the second time with a 2-1 victory over Portsmouth in 1934.

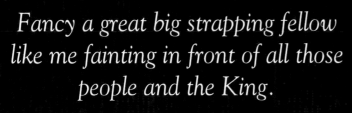

Cowan Makes Good His Promise

The 1933/4 season saw Wild's men improve in the League and again thrive in the FA Cup – a competition the Blues were rapidly making their own. Driven on by skipper Sam Cowan, City saw off Blackburn, Hull and Sheffield Wednesday before taking on Stoke City at Maine Road. It was a game that would be etched into the record books as 84,569 fans crammed into the Blues' home ground to see the game. Stoke had a young Stanley Matthews in their team, but it was Eric Brook who won the day for the Blues scoring the only goal of the match. Then it was on to the semi-final for a third successive year to face cup favourites Aston Villa. Three goals in five first-half minutes settled the tie by the break with City 4-0 to the good. Fred Tilson bagged four on the day as City routed Villa 6-1 – this was a team with a mission and the chance to avenge Portsmouth, who had pipped them to promotion by the slenderest of margins seven years earlier, was too good to turn down. In the final, Pompey employed roughhouse tactics to try and shake City out of their stride, with Tilson and Herd the target of some nasty challenges, but it was Portsmouth who led 1-0 at the interval. Cowan roared his team-mates to show the spirit needed to become champions and it worked wonders as the brilliant Tilson scored two second-half goals to win the game and the FA Cup for City 2-1. Sam Cowan, just as he had predicted 12 months earlier, lifted the trophy to the jubilant hordes from Manchester.

—LEGENDS—

Peter Doherty

FOOTBALL
—STATS—

Peter Doherty

Name: Peter Doherty

Born: 1913

Died: 1990

Playing career: 1933–51

Clubs: Blackpool, Manchester City, Derby County, Huddersfield Town, Doncaster Rovers

City appearances: 133

Goals: 81

Described in reverent tones by those who are old enough to remember him, Peter Doherty was among the finest players ever to pull on a Manchester City shirt – some say *the* finest. The Irish inside-forward was one of the legends of the game and a master tactician on the pitch. Doherty excelled at dribbling, tackling, passing and heading, and delighted the City fans with his endless energy. He signed in 1936 for £10,000 – a club record – and was the star of the Championship-winning side the following season, scoring 32 goals in 45 matches. Doherty was part of the team that followed up the League title with relegation – despite having scored more goals than anybody else had achieved. Only City could do such a thing. The Second World War stole seven years from Doherty, as it did from all footballers throughout the world, though he still played 89 times, scoring 60 goals during wartime for the club. If those were added to his official total, he would have scored 141 goals in just 222 games. Peter died in April 1990. A commemorative plaque has been placed in his native Ireland.

Champions at Last!

In new signing Peter Doherty, the Blues had managed to capture one of the game's brightest talents for £10,000 – a huge fee at the time. His influence in the coming years would more than justify the investment. The 1936/7 season was wonderful for City, but it began poorly with only three wins in their first 14 games, including a first Manchester derby defeat since 1931. Doherty was beginning to show he was a class act, and with Eric Brook, Fred Tilson and Alec Herd, they were all finding the net on a regular basis. Again the crowds at Maine Road were huge: 64,682 witnessed Herd score the only goal of the return derby. Wild's men were on a roll going into the New Year and by March they were on course for a League and Cup double, while United were heading for Division Two – surely a dream come true for any Blue! As the season progressed, City recorded a notable double over Liverpool, winning 5-0 at Anfield and thrashing them 5-1 three days later at Maine Road. Almost 75,000 saw Arsenal leave Moss Side the victims of a rare League double in April and with two games to go, the Blues had the chance to win the title on their own ground with the visit of Sheffield Wednesday.

It was a champion's performance, too, that City served up for the gathered 55,000 as Brook and Tilson gave the hosts a 2-0 lead. Then Doherty added a superb third before the break and despite the visitors pulling one back in the second half, the lethal Brook added a late fourth to seal a wonderful day's work and the League Championship trophy was deservedly City's for the first time in their history. Across the city, United slipped into Division Two and sank further into the sizeable shadow being cast across from Maine Road.

RIGHT: The brilliant Frank Swift was one of the main reasons City became so powerful in the 1930s – a giant of a man, he became a legend for club and country.

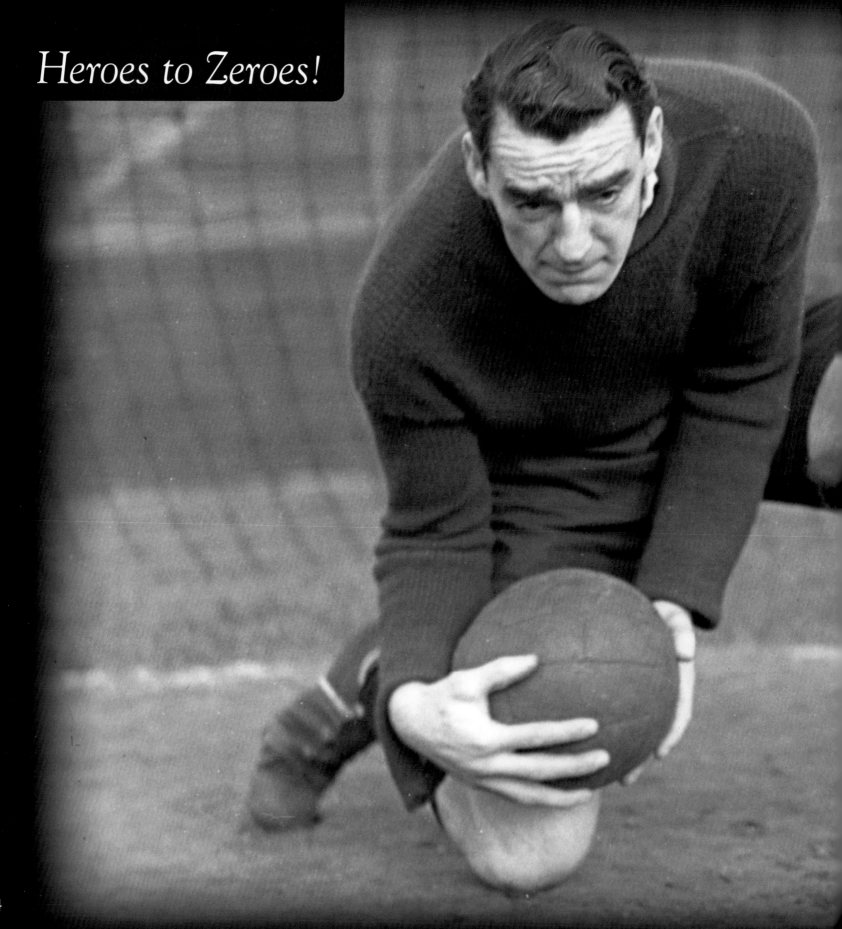

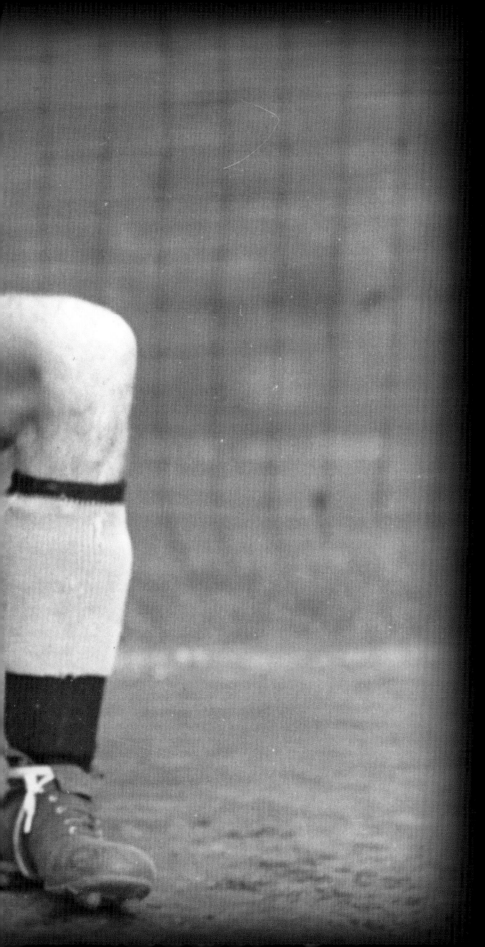

The League champions began in fearsome form at Maine Road, winning six and drawing one of their opening seven home games, scoring 17 and conceding four, but away from home it was the opposite relegation form – losing seven and drawing three of the first 10 away trips. It was a crazy season and when City's home form began to stutter, the side sank towards the foot of the table. It was inexplicable. This was virtually the same side that had swept all before them on the way to becoming champions, but only occasionally were they able to click into gear, hammering opponents when they did.

A run of four defeats going into the New Year was ended with successive away wins – 4-1 at Leicester City and 7-1 at Derby County – but then another slump in form followed and the Blues fans realized the unthinkable was possible as the champs turned chumps and nosedived towards Division Two.

Despite a resounding 6-2 win at home to Leeds in the penultimate game, City still needed something from their final game of the season away to Huddersfield Town. The home side had just lost the FA Cup final and needed a win themselves to stay up. In a tight match, Herd hit the bar but the Blues' luck was out and 12 minutes from time, Town struck the winner. The City players returned to the dressing room not knowing if they had been relegated or not. They needed at least one of Grimsby, Birmingham, Portsmouth or Stoke to have failed to win to survive on goal average, but as the results filtered through, all four had won their games. City, defending champions no less, were relegated as the division's top scorers and just to rub salt in the gaping wounds, United had gained promotion on the final day. What a difference 12 months had made!

LEFT: Even Frank Swift couldn't prevent reigning First Division champions City being relegated in a bizarre 1937/8 campaign.

–LEGENDS–

Frank Swift

One of the club's all-time greats, Frank Swift spent his entire playing career with City and only the outbreak of the Second World War prevented him from being the club's record appearance holder. He spent 16 years with City before his tragic death in 1958. He had to wait as a succession of keepers got their chance and failed until he finally made his debut on Christmas Day 1933, conceding four goals at Derby. The following day, his 20th birthday, he kept a clean sheet in a 2-0 win. Swift then embarked on a run of more than 200 consecutive matches. Such was his importance to the team, when he did miss a game, City lost 6-1 at home to Millwall. The war cost Swift six years of League football, though he was still the first choice for club and country after hostilities ended and played his last game for City in 1949. He was succeeded by Bert Trautmann and then moved into journalism – a role that would lead to tragic consequences when he was asked to cover a Manchester United game overseas and he died in the Munich air disaster.

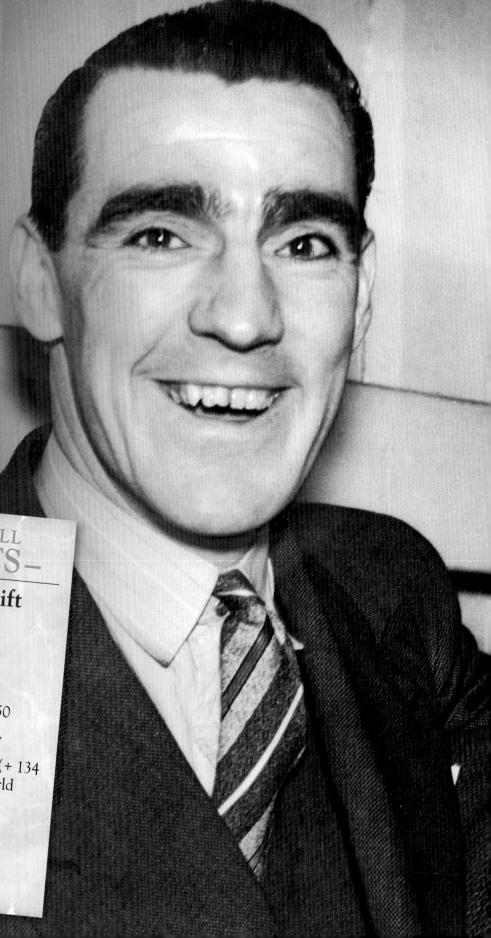

FOOTBALL
–STATS–

Frank Swift

Name: Frank Swift

Born: 1913

Died: 1958

Playing career: 1933–50

Club: Manchester City

City appearances: 376 (+ 134 during the Second World War)

Goals: 0

Frank was a giant in goal – he had a habit of making full-sized nets look like children's goals!

Manchester – a City United

Plans for a return to top-flight football became the least of many City fans' worries when after just three games of the 1939/40 season, war broke out with Germany. League football was suspended as the nation dug in for a long battle and a number of regional divisions were hastily organized, but they were little more than friendly games watched by a handful of fans. On 11th March 1941, Old Trafford scored a direct hit from a German bomb rendering United's home unsafe for the public.

City offered to share Maine Road and the Reds, now managed by former Blue Matt Busby, were grateful of their neighbours' generosity and accepted. In October 1943, England – with City goalkeeper Frank Swift in goal and future boss Joe Mercer playing – defeated Scotland 8-0 in front of around 60,000 fans as the war raged on. Wilf Wild continued as boss as City played in the North Regional League with a bewildering number of players representing the club. League football and D-Day were still several years away.

ABOVE: Old Trafford is bombed during the Second World War leading to a ground-share with City.

Eric Westwood enjoys a spot of extra training.

Return of a Hero

The sterling service of Wilf Wild – perhaps the only man who could have steered the club through such an awful period – began to show the signs of stresses and strain. Though the Blues began well, by November Wild had decided to concentrate on the sizeable administrative role behind the scenes at Maine Road and the City directors sought a former player to restore their club's fortunes. Sam Cowan, hero of the 1930s and former FA Cup-winning skipper, was now running a successful physiotherapy practice in Hove near Brighton. He accepted the offer of becoming City's new manager, but chose to commute from his home on the south coast rather than relocate to Manchester.

Cowan officially took over in the first week of December 1946 and the Blues embarked on an amazing run under the new boss, remaining unbeaten in his first 18 League games. With an already solid foundation, City were now firmly on course for First Division football again with future Liverpool boss Joe Fagan settling in well in the side.

By the final match of the campaign, City had won the title by four points and were back where they belonged. For Sam Cowan, however, it was the end to his brief managerial career. The directors felt his commuting and refusal to move north made his role untenable and Cowan returned to his practice in Hove. It was a huge disappointment to the fans who believed Cowan would have led the club to even greater heights.

RIGHT: The 1947 Manchester derby at Maine Road – the captains shake hands before playing out a 0-0 draw in front of a huge crowd of 78,000 people.

May 1947: A smile for the photographer from Roy Clarke, the Cardiff and Welsh international outside-left, after signing for City at Maine Road. Also in the picture is long-serving club secretary Wilf Wild.

Blues Continue to Pack Them In

34

City take on United at a packed Maine Road in September 1947. Crowds in excess of 60,000 were not uncommon and the Blues set a provincial crowd record when more than 84,000 squeezed in for the visit of Stoke City in the FA Cup in 1934.

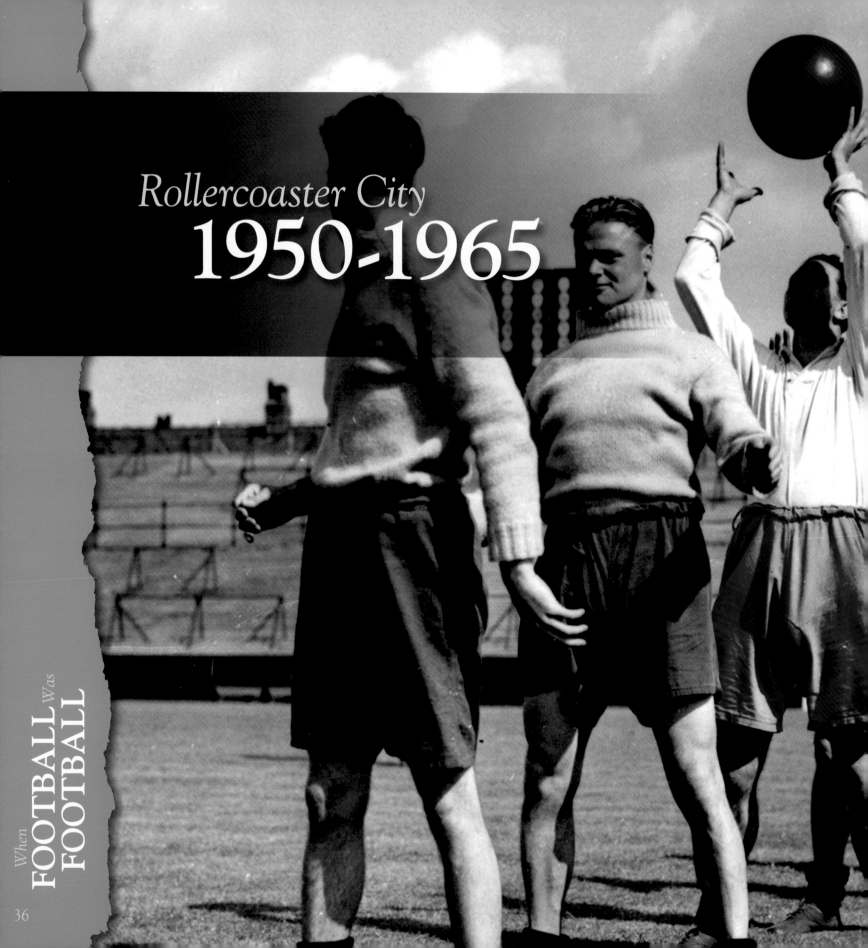

Rollercoaster City
1950-1965

Training sessions were often held at Maine Road, particularly in pre-season. The kit worn is not dissimilar to a PE kit and would be expected to last all year – a world away from today's seemingly limitless supply of tracksuits and various other items.

1950 City are relegated from the top flight after just three years in Division One. 1951 Les McDowall celebrates his first season in charge at Maine Road by guiding the Blues to the runners-up spot in Division Two. 1955 City reach their fourth FA Cup final, but lose 3-1 to Newcastle United. 1956 City finish fourth in Division One – their highest position since winning the lead 19 years earlier. Also, for the second time in club history, the Blues return the following season on the promise of their captain – Roy Paul in this case – to lift the Cup, beating Birmingham 2-1 in the 'Trautmann final' in which City's heroic German keeper breaks his neck diving at the feet of Peter Murphy. 1958 City finish fifth in Division One after scoring 104 goals and conceding 100. 1963 Les McDowall is replaced by George Poyser after City are relegated to Division Two. 1965 Joe Mercer appointed manager with Malcolm Allison employed as his assistant.

LEFT: June 1950: Eric Westwood returns to pre-season training early in preparation for the 1950/1 campaign. These extra sessions pay off, as City win promotion back to Division One at the first attempt.

PLEASE HAVE CORRECT MONEY READY

ADMISSION FIRST TEAM I SECOND TEAM 9ᵈ

ABOVE: Matchday in 1950 and the gates at Maine Road open early. With almost more policemen on duty than spectators, people felt comfortable enough to leave their bikes leaning against the wall. There is also a healthy presence of women and kids for what was believed to be anything but a family game.

A Legend is Born

Bert Trautmann in action against Wolverhampton Wanderers, August 1951. The big German keeper had to fight to win the respect of not only the City fans but the entire nation, with the wounds of the Second World War still raw. Trautmann had been spotted playing for non-League St Helen's Town and was the perfect replacement for the legendary Frank Swift – in fact, there probably wasn't another goalkeeper in the world who could have filled Swift's boots in such impressive fashion.

> *There's no war in this dressing room.*
>
> Eric Westwood welcomes Trautmann to the team

The Show Must Go On!

Ground staff attempt to thaw out Maine Road the day before an important home game in January 1953. Braziers filled with hot coal make little impression, so straw was laid to cover the pitch from another merciless frost. Oh, for undersoil heating!

In 1950 Les McDowall had taken the reins from John Thomson who had failed to build on the momentum achieved by Sam Cowan during the 1946/7 campaign. Finishes of seventh, tenth and twenty-first under Thomson meant McDowall had to start life in Division Two. A former City captain who had been unfortunate to join just before the war – the conflict had taken up a large chunk of his time at the club – McDowall soon settled into his new role by taking City back up to Division One at the first attempt, but the next two campaigns were a struggle with the Blues just avoiding the drop in three successive campaigns before the introduction of forward Don Revie, a £25,000-buy from Hull City. Revie scored few goals, but his effect on the team was impressive as a previously ordinary side suddenly challenged for the title and the FA Cup during his first season at Maine Road.

26th March 1955: Roy Clarke sends City to Wembley for the first time in 21 years as the Blues beat Sunderland 1-0 at Villa Park.

Bert Trautmann races through a crowd of well-wishers following City's FA Cup semi-final triumph over Sunderland.

The Revie Plan

Don Revie would become an integral part of Les McDowall's City team of the mid-1950s. The Blues developed a plan that was unique by employing Revie as a deep-lying forward who would pick up the ball more or less in midfield and then distribute or attack from distance. Defenders found him impossible to mark and the 'Revie Plan' was cited as one of the main reasons City returned to Wembley in 1956.

ABOVE: Don Revie knocks the ball down to a team-mate during a January 1955 Manchester derby. Note the old roof on the Main Stand and the state of the churned-up Maine Road pitch.

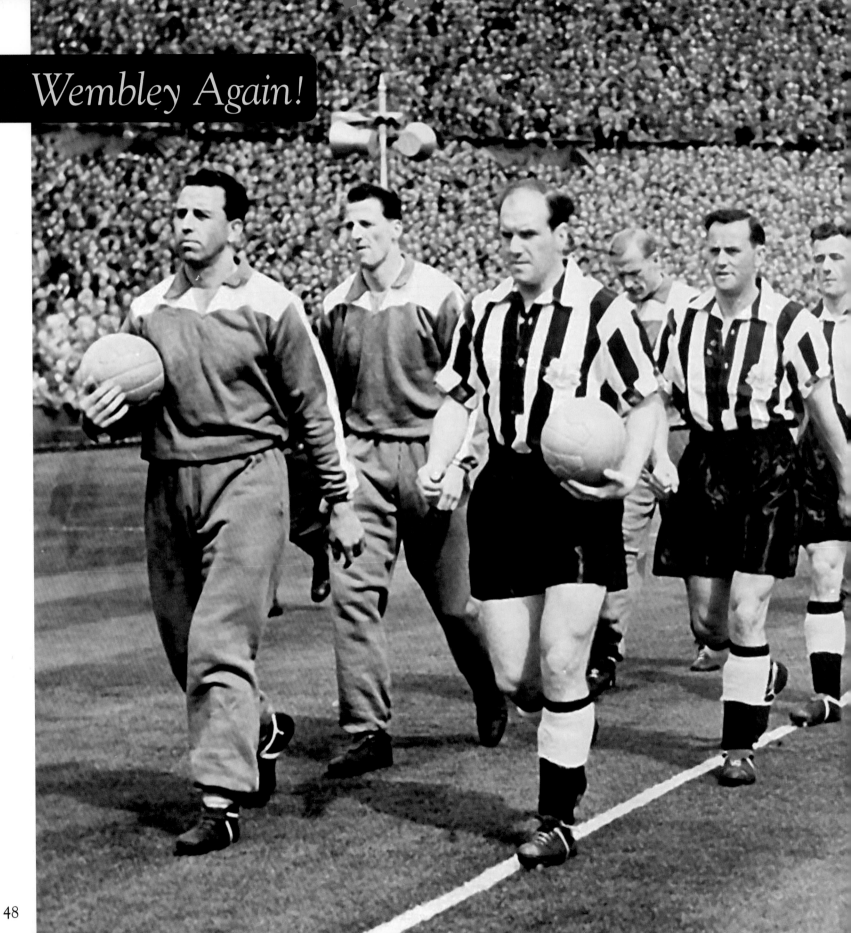

LEFT: Newcastle and City, led by skipper Roy Paul, walk out for the 1955 FA Cup final. It wouldn't be the Blues' day with the Magpies winning 3-1 to grasp what would prove to be their last major trophy to date. Blues' skipper Paul, just like Sam Cowan 32 years earlier, had vowed to return and lift the following year...

BELOW: The Duke of Edinburgh shakes hands with the City players before the start of the game.

–LEGENDS–

Roy Paul

Roy Paul was Manchester City's very own Captain Fantastic. An inspirational figure to colleagues and fans alike, Paul captained the Blues to the 1955 FA Cup final, where they lost to Newcastle United, and then vowed to return to win the cup the next year. The former coal miner drove the Blues on to the 1956 FA Cup final and this time City were victorious over Birmingham City. Paul had arrived from Swansea Town in 1950 and was versatile in that he could play anywhere across the back line. A true 'Roy of the Rovers'-type player, Paul is one of the greatest captains the club has ever had and he was only the second Welshman to skipper the Blues to FA Cup glory – the first being Billy Meredith. Paul left for Worcester City in June 1957 after clocking up nearly 300 matches for City. He died in the spring of 2002.

> *We'll be back next year, but next time we'll win it.*
>
> Roy Paul

FOOTBALL –STATS–

Roy Paul

Name: Roy Paul

Born: 1913

Died: 2002

Playing career: 1946–60

Clubs: Swansea, Manchester City, Worcester

City appearances: 293

Goals: 5

City Captain Roy Paul looks on (right of ref) as City take on Manchester United in 1955.

Return Ticket to Wembley

The City players dusted themselves down from the disappointment of losing the 1955 FA Cup final against Newcastle and began the 1955/6 season like a team with a severe hangover. Two 2-2 draws and a 7-2 hammering at Wolves must have left boss Les McDowall wondering where his side were heading. It was only a temporary blip, however, as skipper Roy Paul set about waking his team-mates up to the job in hand with great effect with a 1-0 win over United in front of nearly 60,000 fans at Maine Road. By Christmas the Blues were sitting in mid-table looking at another unremarkable season. At least Paul had the FA Cup to aim for and he had the promise of returning to Wembley as champions to fulfil.

City had drawn Blackpool at home and were level at 1-1 when the game was abandoned due to severe weather. The match was replayed four days later, with Bobby Johnstone and Jackie Dyson scoring the goals in a 2-1 win. Southend-away was a tight-fought tie, with Joe Hayes scoring the only goal of the game at Roots Hall. So far, so good for Paul's glorious prophecy!

The Blues' League form also picked up and McDowall's men were climbing the table accordingly. A home fifth-round pairing with Second Division Liverpool seemed a comfortable draw and 70,640 fans packed Maine Road to cheer their heroes into the last 16.

The Reds clung on for a 0-0 draw and the prospect of a packed Anfield for the replay suddenly looked a daunting proposition until goals from Hayes and Dyson clinched a 2-1 win and a home draw with Everton. Cup fever was gripping the City fans and more than 76,000 watched a 2-1 home win with goals from Hayes and Johnstone. City beat Everton 3-0 at Maine Road in the League four days later, but just over 15,000 turned out for that game.

Two games from glory, Roy Paul was not about to let his dream slip away and he was inspirational in the semi-final as City beat Spurs 1-0 to return to Wembley for the second successive year. Their opponents would be Birmingham City who had already beaten and drawn City earlier in the League campaign...

BELOW: City, the beaten 1955 FA Cup finalists, return fresh from their summer break ready to embark on what would be a memorable campaign in the League and the FA Cup. From left to right: Roy Paul, Roy Clarke, Paddy Fagan, Bobby Johnstone, Joe Hayes, Roy Little, Ken Barnes, Don Revie, Jimmy Meadows, Bert Trautmann and Dave Ewing.

BELOW INSET: Johnny Hart watches on as his team-mates complete another lap of the Maine Road pitch. Hart was recovering from a broken leg.

Legends Together

Two of City's greatest goalkeepers, Bert Trautmann and Frank Swift, chat on a sunny afternoon at Maine Road. The retired Swift was working as a journalist and was interviewing his successor prior to the 1956 FA Cup final against Birmingham. In Swift and Trautmann, over a 30-year period, City had the best goalkeepers in the country, if not Europe, with both men clocking up a combined appearance total in excess of 1,000 games.

Ladies Day

The WAGS of the day prepare to depart by train for London. With their husbands and fiancés about to contest the FA Cup final, the ladies had to keep their distance until the match had been played. From left to right: Mrs D Ewing, Mrs J Meadows, Miss Metcalfe (soon to be Mrs R Little), Miss Bradley (to be Mrs J Hayes), Mrs P Fagan, Mrs B Spurdle, Mrs D Revie, Mrs R Paul, Mrs J Beeston, Mrs L Barnett and Mrs R Clarke.

Moments Before Kick-off...

A rare shot of the two teams preparing to walk out of the tunnel at Wembley to contest the 1956 Cup final. From the glamour and glitz associated with the final tie, note the grimy, miserable surrounds of a stadium that was still only 23 years old.

The Trautmann Final

LEFT: The Duke of Edinburgh meets the City players before the match kicks off – with Prince Philip being of German descent, it would have been interesting to have heard what his conversation with Bert Trautmann, who is seen graciously bowing to HRH, was about.

The team to face Birmingham had a good solid look about it, but a late injury to Billy Spurdle meant a chance for Don Revie to play. McDowall had employed the 'Revie Plan' in the final against Newcastle and had been roundly criticized for doing so, but he was determined to prove the doubters wrong.

Hayes gave City a dream start with a goal after two minutes, but Kinsey equalized for Birmingham after a quarter of an hour. Revie was causing all kinds of problems for the Midland club and he again played a part in City's second goal, midway through the second half, scored by Dyson.

Two minutes later and City were 3-1 up through Bobby Johnstone and the victory was effectively sealed. But there was more drama to come. On 75 minutes Bert Trautmann made a typically brave save at the feet of Brum striker Murphy who caught the big German's neck with his knee. Trautmann was treated for several minutes before soldiering on in great agony.

With no substitutes in those days, had Trautmann left the field – as he should have done – City could well have still lost the game with no goalkeeper. Trautmann had broken his neck, but stayed until the final whistle having conceded no more goals.

RIGHT: Jack Dyson puts City 2-1 up following a delightful move involving Don Revie, Bobby Johnstone and Ken Barnes. Johnstone made it 3-1 two minutes later to give the Blues the breathing space needed.

RIGHT INSET: City skipper Roy Paul revels in the moment, his prophecy realized on an unforgettable day for the club.

61

A Legend is Born

Still unaware he had broken his neck, Bert Trautmann joins Don Revie in the dressing-room celebrations after the match. X-rays would later reveal the Blues' keeper could have been paralysed had he sustained another knock during the final minutes of the game, making his bravery even more incredible.

Still in great discomfort, Trautmann visits a specialist the day after the final. He was told by a doctor at St George's Hospital, London, that he merely had a crick in his neck which would go away in time. Three days later, he obtained a second opinion from a doctor at Manchester Royal Infirmary. An X-ray revealed he had dislocated five vertebrae in his neck, the second of which was cracked in two. The third vertebra had wedged against the second, preventing further damage that could have cost him his life.

ABOVE: Roy Paul lifts the FA Cup – but this time at the civic reception at the Manchester Town Hall held in the team's honour.

THE CLASS OF 1956

Seated, from left to right: Paddy Fagan, Joe Hayes, Don Revie, Bobby Johnstone and Roy Clarke. Standing, from left to right: Les McDowall (manager), Ken Barnes, Roy Paul, Bert Trautmann, Jimmy Meadows, Dave Ewing, Roy Little and Laurie Barnett.

Tough Times Ahead for Blues...

The Blues celebrated their FA Cup triumph throughout the summer of 1956 and enjoyed a tour of Manchester in front of their ecstatic supporters. The honeymoon ended on the opening day of the new season, however, with a 5-1 defeat at Wolves. In fact, it was a pretty awful season for the club who gave up their hold on the FA Cup at the first attempt by losing 5-4 at home to Newcastle United. Manchester United completed the double over City and manager Les McDowall must have been scratching his head at his team's inconsistency.

City finished just above the relegation places in 18th, with Bobby Johnstone top-scoring with 16 strikes from 31 League games. Bert Trautmann had made an amazing recovery from his broken neck and played every game of the second half of the season.

The 1957/8 campaign proved more fruitful, but with Don Revie now departed, McDowall attempted the 'Marsden Plan' that resulted in disastrous losses of 6-1 at Preston and 9-2 at West Brom in successive games. City keeper Savage, standing in for Trautmann, had come in for some severe punishment and left the club shortly afterwards. Another FA Cup drubbing of 5-1 at West Brom meant the Baggies had scored 14 goals in two home games against the Blues in just over four months. It was an incredible season for City at both ends of the pitch. By the end of a crazy season, City had scored 104 and conceded 100 goals – the only time this feat has ever happened before or since.

The Lawman Arrives

Finishing in fifth position in 1957/8 was to be the last time Les McDowall would steer his troops into the top 10 under his command as several seasons of average football followed, with finishes of 20th, 15th, 13th, 12th and, in 1962/3, 21st resulting in relegation. At least he oversaw the purchase of highly rated young Scottish striker Denis Law, who was to become one of soccer's hottest properties over the next 12 months.

For McDowall, who had been in charge for 13 years, relegation spelled the end of his tenure at Maine Road. He had never really managed to make City a major force in that time, with the 1956 FA Cup success his only real triumph. The side was in a transitional period between a crop of emerging youngsters and a group of experienced pros coming to the end of their careers. George Poyser was installed as the new City boss – but things were about to get even bleaker.

LEFT: March 1960 – Denis Law signs from Huddersfield for a bargain £55,000 – still a British transfer record at the time. Skipper Ken Barnes shows the young striker his new shirt.

RIGHT: It's a dog's life! At his digs in Withington, Manchester, Denis Law reflects on the day his historic double hat-trick was wiped from the records. After scoring all six in City's 6-2 lead at Luton, the elements conspired to make the pitch unplayable and with 69 minutes played, the match was abandoned. The rearranged game saw City lose 3-1, with Law again on the score-sheet.

Trautmann's Record Testimonial

14th April 1964: Bert Trautmann leads out the combined City and United team against an All Star International XI led by Jimmy Armfield for his testimonial match. More than 47,000 packed into Maine Road to pay their respects to the City legend, though many believe the gate was nearer 60,000 – a gauge of his immense standing among the supporters. City's average crowd during the 1963/4 season was less than 22,000. For the record, Trautmann's Manchester team won 5-4.

> *Words failed me. The City fans had always been amazing to me but to see so many come to my benefit match sent shivers down my spine.*
>
> Bert Trautmann

ABOVE: Trautmann celebrates with a swig of champagne with, among others, Manchester United's Bobby Charlton (second from right).

Sacked manager George Poyser relaxes in the sunshine with a glass of beer and his pipe at his home in Sale after a disappointing 11th-place finish in Division Two. The style of football and poor crowds convinced the board it was time for a change at the top, though few could imagine the change in fortunes City were about to enjoy.

George Poyser had been the natural choice to take over from Les McDowall, but try as he might, he couldn't arrest the club's fortunes. After travelling the length and breadth of the country watching players during his role as assistant, he made a couple of intelligent signings, including Derek Kevan and Jimmy Murray, and for the first six months in charge, things seemed to be on the up. City were challenging for promotion and were in the semi-final of the League Cup, but a sixth-place finish was ultimately disappointing. The Murray-Kevan partnership had been an outstanding success, however, with the pair netting 51 goals between them during their first season at Maine Road. The following campaign, however, saw crowds dwindling and a mid-table finish – if the board didn't act quickly, the Blues were in danger of drifting even further down the table and so Poyser was sacked. It was time to think outside of the box and the City board felt they knew who was the perfect man to lead the club back to the top flight...

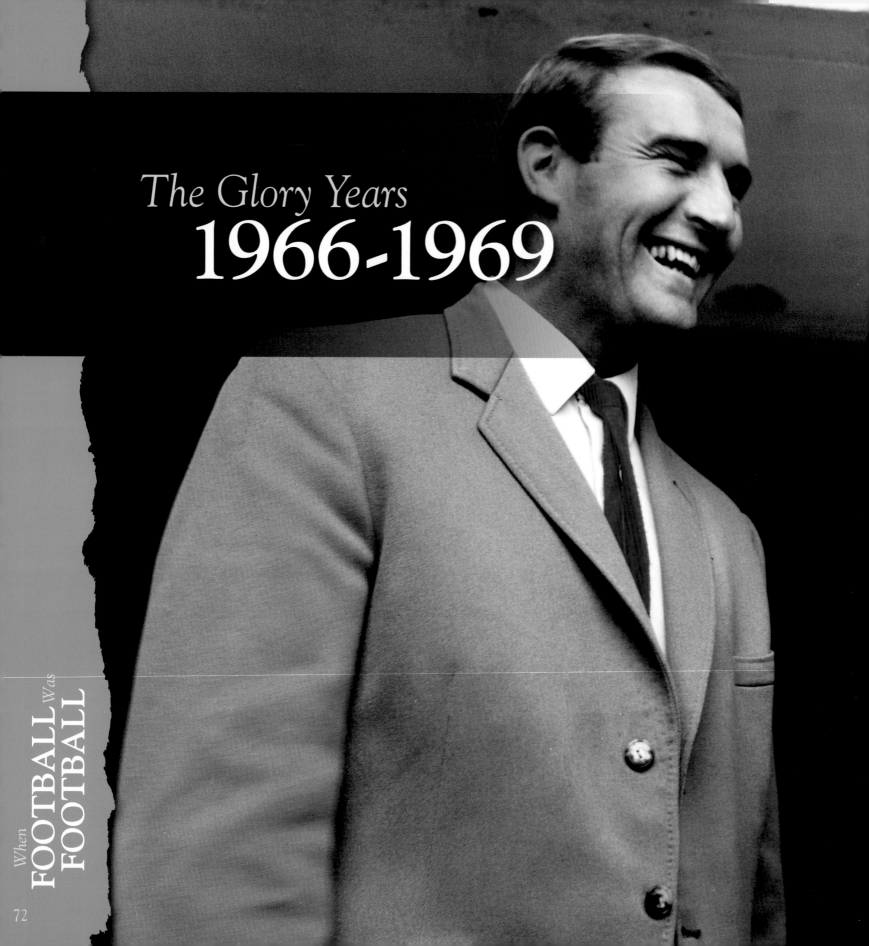

The Glory Years
1966-1969

Former Aston Villa manager Joe Mercer had been forced out of Villa Park due to ill-health and many wondered if he would ever return to football. Despite being given a clean bill of health by doctors, the Villa board sacked him and he found himself out of work for one of the first times in his life. Villa's error was to be City's gain and when the Blues offered him the chance of resurrecting a fallen giant, he grabbed the opportunity with both hands. He wasted no time in signing Plymouth Argyle's highly rated manager Malcolm Allison, making the respected coach his No.2. The pair were the ideal combination of old and new-school thinking and while Mercer projected the perfect image of the club and took care of the administrative side, Allison got to work on the training ground with his revolutionary

1966 City win Second Division and sign Colin Bell and Mike Summerbee. **1967** Tony Book joins City from Plymouth and Francis Lee signs from Bolton for a fee of £60,000. **1968** City win League title for only the second time after pipping Manchester United to the title on the final day of the campaign with a thrilling 4-3 win at Newcastle. City's only ever foray into the European Cup ends with a first-round defeat to Fenerbahce. City record a 6-1 FA Charity Shield win over West Brom. **1969** The Blues edge the 1969 FA Cup final 1-0 thanks to Neil Young's goal against Leicester City.

Malcolm Allison sits on the bench for the first time since his arrival, while as
Joe Mercer sat in the stand during a 2-1 pre-season friendly defeat to Dundee.

New signing Mike Summerbee (front, second from right) is joined by several Manchester United players and Harry Dowd and Johnny Crossan (both to the left of Summerbee) at a model-racing-car competition in Manchester. Summerbee took to the bright city lights of Manchester like the proverbial duck to water following his move from Swindon Town a few months earlier. City were already looking like title candidates by the start of November, having lost just one of their opening 15 League games in Division Two, and by the end of the season had comfortably won the title.

Best of Mates

Majorca 1967: With City regaining their top-flight status after winning the Division Two title, Mike Summerbee soon found a kindred spirit in Manchester United idol George Best. The pair became inseparable and even holidayed together, inevitably attracting plenty of female attention.

Best and Summerbee opened a fashion boutique in the city centre in 1967. The Edwardian was a high-class menswear store that attracted celebrities and sports stars from all over the northwest.

Inside the boutique with Buzzer and Best. The champagne lifestyle of both players was repeated on the pitch, where both City and United were challenging for the League title, with the Blues in particular playing with the panache and style for which the supporters had yearned.

—LEGENDS—

Mike Summerbee

Joe Mercer's decision to make Mike Summerbee his first signing as Manchester City manager prior to the 1965/6 season was arguably also one of his best. The Cheltenham-born winger arrived for just £31,000 from Swindon Town, upping his wage from £35 to £40. Summerbee proved an instant hit with City fans and fitted perfectly into a side destined for promotion from the Second Division during his first campaign at Maine Road.

He played in all 52 games in League and Cup competitions, scoring 10 goals as the Blues returned to the top flight after a three-year absence. Summerbee added a new dimension to the team with his trickery and ability to get to the by-line and whip over wonderful crosses. He played 50 games in all competitions, scoring 19 goals as City went on to win the League title in 1968 – a fantastic return.

Like many City stars of the era and since, his haul of eight England caps was scant reward for his consistency and performances at club level that merited at least three times that amount if not more. He laid on the winning goal for Neil Young in the 1969 FA Cup final and was also instrumental in the 1970 League Cup final win over West Brom a year later – sustaining a hairline fracture of the leg during the game, which meant he missed the European Cup Winners' Cup final just seven weeks later.

Buzzer continued to give excellent service for many years at Maine Road, becoming skipper for the 1973/4 season and leading his team out at Wembley for the 1974 League Cup final against Wolves, though he had to settle for a runners-up medal on the day. When Tony Book became manager in 1974, he accepted Burnley's bid of £25,000, allowing one of the most distinguished No.7s in the club's history to move on.

FOOTBALL
–STATS–

Mike Summerbee

Name: Mike Summerbee

Born: 1942

Signed: 1965, Swindon Town

Playing career: 1959–79

Clubs: Swindon, Manchester City, Burnley, Blackpool, Stockport

City appearances: 449 (+ 3 as a substitute)

Goals: 68

The Thinker

Always happy to pose for pictures and able to provide wonderful quotes, Malcolm Allison was rarely out of the back pages in the late 1960s. Handsome, brash and confident, he lived the champagne lifestyle off the pitch, but on it he was as dedicated, intelligent a coach as you could possibly find. His players would have run through brick walls for him. He was years ahead of his time with his thinking and methods, and it was City who reaped the benefit.

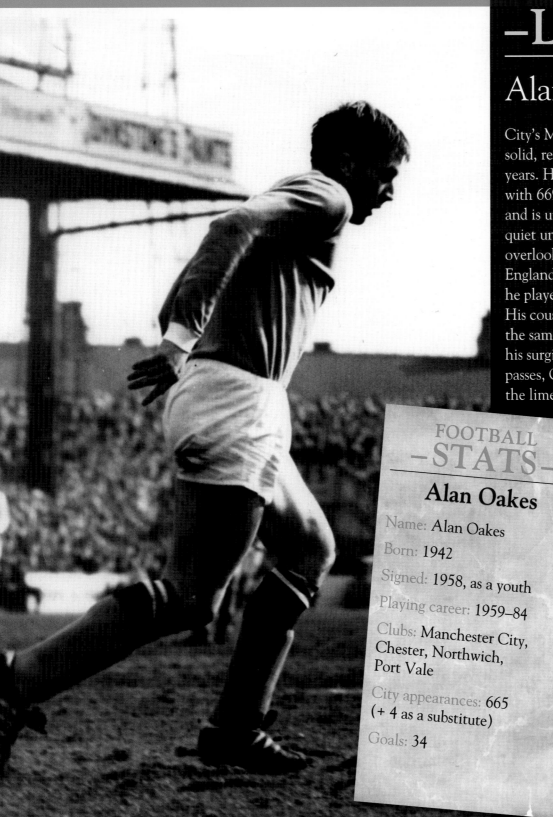

–LEGENDS–

Alan Oakes

City's Mr Dependable, Alan Oakes gave solid, reliable service to the club for over 18 years. He is the record-appearance holder, with 669 competitive starts under his belt, and is unlikely ever to be surpassed. He was a quiet unassuming player who was criminally overlooked at all international levels for England, due almost entirely to the fact that he played a similar role to Bobby Moore. His cousin was another unsung hero from the same era, Glyn Pardoe. Best known for his surging runs from deep and penetrative passes, Oakes was happy to let others take the limelight yet was vital to the glorious all-conquering Mercer side of the late 1960s, and the management showed their faith in Oakes by naming him captain for the 1968/9 season. He was also named in the original squad of 40 for the 1970 World Cup, but missed out on a trip to Mexico when the final squad was announced. Consistent right up until the end of his days at Maine Road, he was named Player of the Year in 1975, just a year before he left City for Chester, where he eventually became player-manager of the club after adding another 211 appearances to his career total. He had made over 900 appearances for the Blues at all levels.

FOOTBALL –STATS–

Alan Oakes

Name: Alan Oakes

Born: 1942

Signed: 1958, as a youth

Playing career: 1959–84

Clubs: Manchester City, Chester, Northwich, Port Vale

City appearances: 665 (+ 4 as a substitute)

Goals: 34

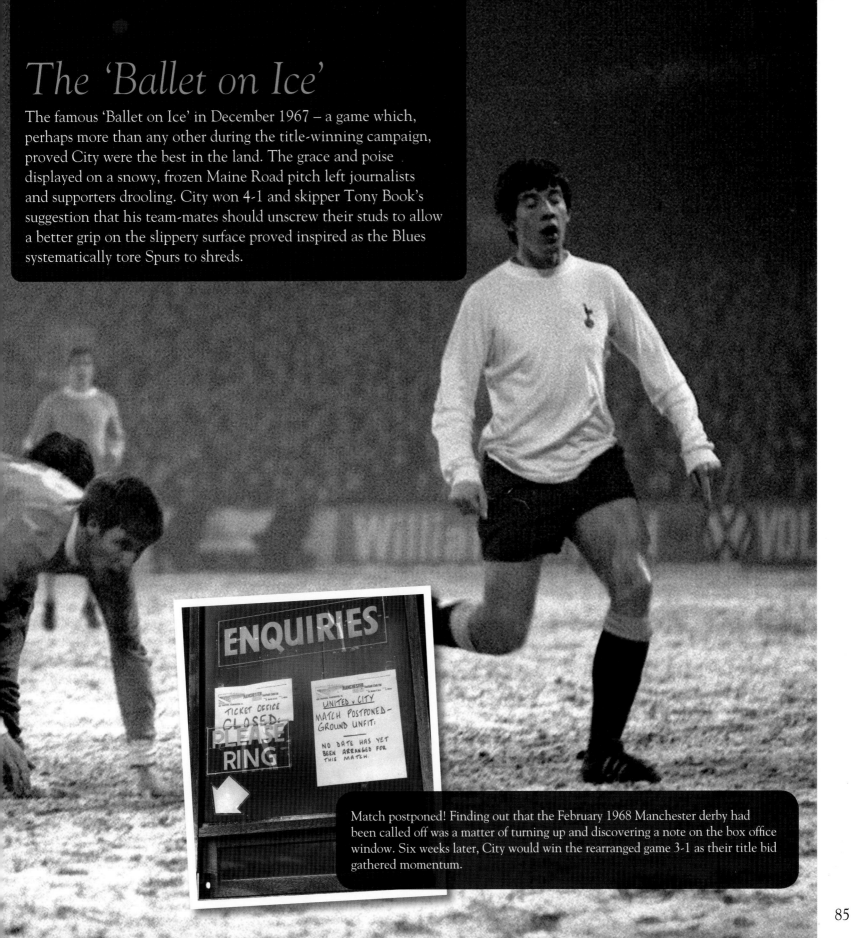

The 'Ballet on Ice'

The famous 'Ballet on Ice' in December 1967 – a game which, perhaps more than any other during the title-winning campaign, proved City were the best in the land. The grace and poise displayed on a snowy, frozen Maine Road pitch left journalists and supporters drooling. City won 4-1 and skipper Tony Book's suggestion that his team-mates should unscrew their studs to allow a better grip on the slippery surface proved inspired as the Blues systematically tore Spurs to shreds.

ENQUIRIES

MANCHESTER Football Club Ltd

TICKET OFFICE
CLOSED.
PLEASE
RING

MANCHESTER Football Club Ltd

UNITED v CITY
MATCH POSTPONED –
GROUND UNFIT.

NO DATE HAS YET
BEEN ARRANGED FOR
THIS MATCH.

Match postponed! Finding out that the February 1968 Manchester derby had been called off was a matter of turning up and discovering a note on the box office window. Six weeks later, City would win the rearranged game 3-1 as their title bid gathered momentum.

Brilliant City!

What was to be a glorious period for City began in the 1967/8 season with a 0-0 draw at home to Liverpool and was followed by successive defeats at Southampton and Stoke. One point from a possible six hardly had the Blues' odds for the title slashed in half. But somewhere along the line things clicked into place and City won their next five games on the bounce. The Mercer-Allison partnership was a dream pairing, but there was still one piece of the jigsaw missing.

Successive defeats to United, Arsenal and Sunderland had the management team scratching their heads, but a new signing would add the finishing touch to this magnificent team. City splashed £60,000 on the highly rated Bolton youngster Francis Lee and it was the stocky Westhoughton-born striker who helped the Blues move to the next level required of champions.

Lee's first 11 League appearances for City resulted in eight wins and three draws. He also scored eight times as his new club raced towards the top of the table.

Mike Summerbee, Colin Bell, Neil Young and Tony Coleman and new boy Francis Lee were a daunting prospect for any defence to face and as City left the pitch at Reading, having won an FA Cup replay 7-0, the PA announced that the home fans had "just seen the best team in England".

The New Year began with six League wins in seven as the Blues kept the pressure on their title challengers. All the forwards and midfielders were scoring freely and the defence rarely let in more than one goal. Defeat at Leeds in March was followed with a triumphant 3-1 win at United and it was perhaps this victory that would prove as crucial as any on the run-in.

The next five games brought delight at home, with wins over Chelsea and West Ham, but despair away with two defeats and a draw and no goals whatsoever. If the jitters were setting in, it was incredibly bad timing.

With just four fixtures remaining, City had to rely on a scrambled own goal to edge past Sheffield Wednesday at Maine Road 1-0, but the 2-0 home-win four days later over Everton was far more assured. Mercer's men believed they could do it. On the trip to White Hart Lane to face a Spurs team out to avenge their 4-1 thrashing at Maine Road the previous December, christened 'The Ballet on Ice' by the watching media, the Blues turned on an awesome first-half display and were 3-0 up by half-time. The trouble was they had literally run themselves into the ground and Tottenham began to take a grip of the game sensing an unlikely comeback.

As it was, City clung on to win 3-1 and were left with the scenario the whole of Manchester had longed for, with both City and United going into the last day of the season with the potential of winning the title. Liverpool had an outside chance, but it was really all about who would be crowned kings of Manchester.

George Best puts United 1-0 up after just 38 seconds of the March 1968 derby, but City roar back to win 3-1

City, slightly ahead of their deadly rivals United, faced a tough trip to Newcastle United, while United faced Sunderland at Old Trafford. It was the ultimate nerve-shredder for all Mancunians, but particularly the City faithful who knew their team could still produce totally unpredictable displays whenever they pleased. More than 20,000 Blues made the trip to the northeast to cheer their heroes home and were rewarded with an unbelievable match. Summerbee struck City ahead, but the Geordies levelled almost immediately. On the half-hour, Young restored the Blues' lead, but again the home side drew level almost straight away and the teams went in at the break level at 2-2. Back came City, with further goals from Young and Lee giving them the breathing space they desperately needed. Newcastle still pulled one back five minutes from time and came close to levelling before the whistle went for full-time to send the travelling hordes wild with delight. City had won their first title for 30 years and the celebrations lasted long into the summer. The fact that United had lost anyway was irrelevant – nobody was going to steal the thunder of the new champions of England.

Francis Lee puts City 4-2 up at Newcastle on the final day of the 1967/8 campaign. City eventually won 4-3, with Neil Young (2) and Mike Summerbee also on the score-sheet, gaining the two points they needed to win the League title for only the second time. More than 20,000 City fans had flocked to St James' Park to support the team and moments after the final whistle, the majority of them spilled onto the pitch to celebrate.

LEFT: Malcolm Allison's famous "we will terrify Europe" quote.

Plenty to smile about – skipper Tony Book joins Joe Mercer and Malcolm Allison at a cheerful board meeting. With the championship trophy now resting proudly in the club's trophy cabinet, it's not hard to understand why there was so much happiness at Maine Road.

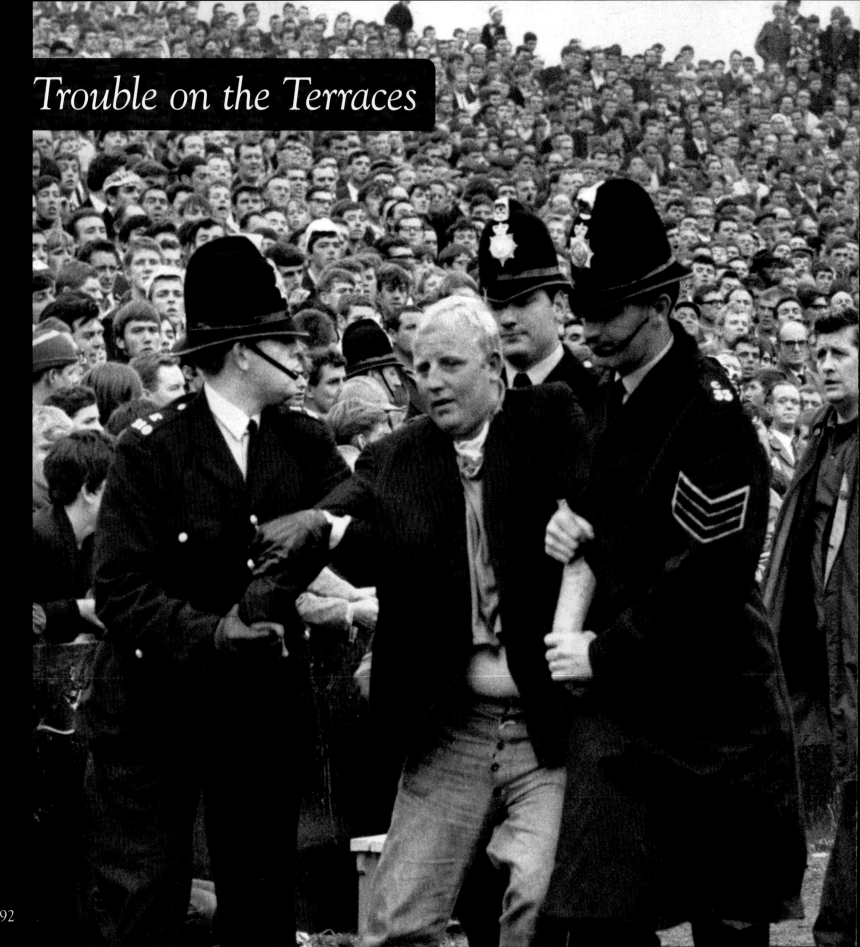

Trouble on the Terraces

Hard as it may seem to believe, the late 1960s saw an upsurge in crowd trouble and where fans of both clubs once stood side by side on the terraces, segregation was mooted for the first time. Trouble was still rare at Maine Road, but this picture shows the days of harmony among football fans were numbered as several Liverpool fans are ejected from the North Stand.

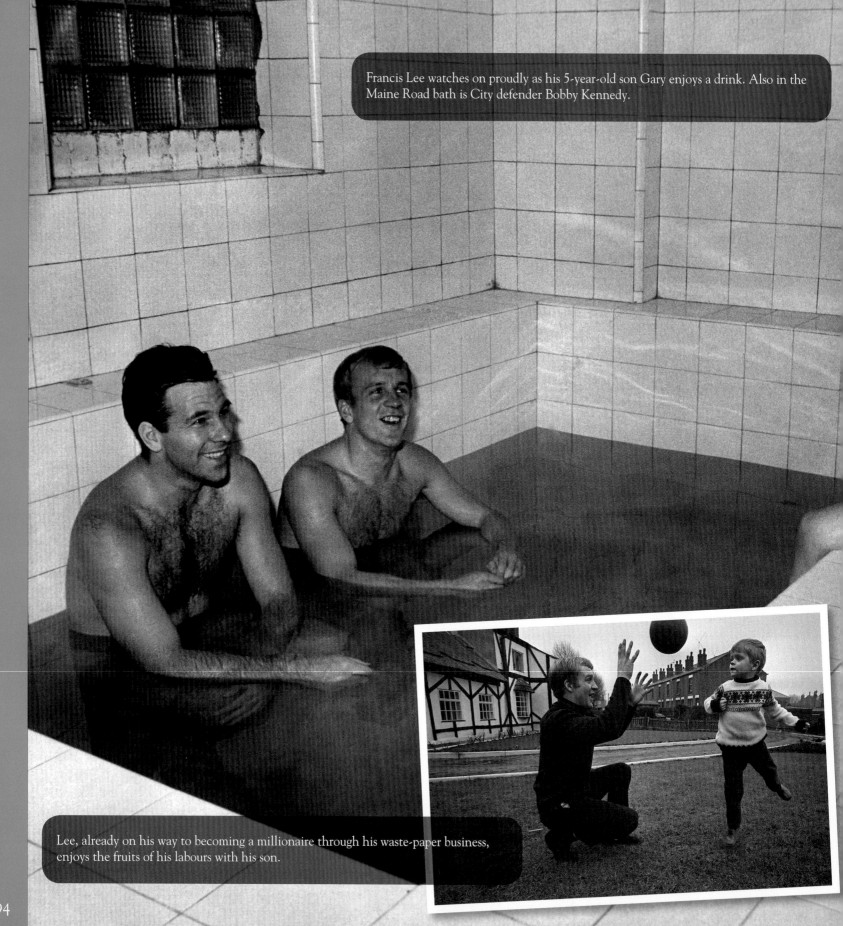

Francis Lee watches on proudly as his 5-year-old son Gary enjoys a drink. Also in the Maine Road bath is City defender Bobby Kennedy.

Lee, already on his way to becoming a millionaire through his waste-paper business, enjoys the fruits of his labours with his son.

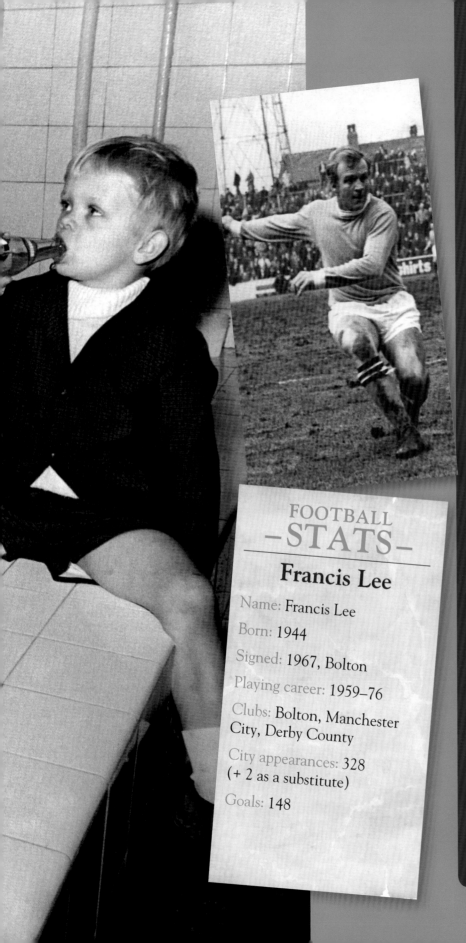

–LEGENDS–

Francis Lee

Francis Lee was signed by Joe Mercer in 1967 in the hope the £60,000 paid to Bolton would help the Blues land the First Division title. The forward had a proven track record at Bolton where he had made his debut aged 16 and had been playing first-team football for seven years. He had also notched a very healthy 92 goals in 132 games for Wanderers. Lee was perfect for the City team and it wasn't too long before the management and supporters realized that the 23-year-old Westhoughton lad was the final piece of Mercer and Allison's intricate jigsaw, with the Blues landing the League title in his first season.

Though physically short and stocky in appearance, Lee was a born winner who never gave less than 100 per cent for his team. He battled for every ball and gave as good as he got – few messed with Franny on the pitch.

Along with Bell and Summerbee, City's star trio became known as the Holy Trinity and inspired more success the following year with a FA Cup final triumph over Leicester. Lee also finished joint top-scorer in the League. A year later and it was a cup double for the Blues as they lifted the League Cup and then the European Cup Winners' Cup in the space of six weeks in 1970. Lee scored the decisive goal in Vienna to secure a 2-1 win and a first major European trophy for the club. He was also deadly from the penalty spot, winning and then dispatching the vast majority himself.

He finished top-scorer again in 1970/1 and had his best ever season for the club in 1971/2, when City almost won the League title, scoring an incredible 35 goals in 46 League and cup games and converting a club record 15 penalties along the way.

FOOTBALL –STATS–

Francis Lee

Name: Francis Lee

Born: 1944

Signed: 1967, Bolton

Playing career: 1959–76

Clubs: Bolton, Manchester City, Derby County

City appearances: 328 (+ 2 as a substitute)

Goals: 148

Blues in Colour

ABOVE: Lee in action against Liverpool.

RIGHT: Colin Bell's diving header can't stop City losing 2-1 to Bill Shankly's Liverpool at Anfield as the title defence gets off to a shaky start.

Buzzer holds back an angry Dave Mackay of Spurs in a heated match at White Hart Lane.

Best Men!

George Best is Mike Summerbee's best man at his wedding at a rainy Church of St Michael and All Angels, Mottram, September 1968.

BELOW: Mike weds 20-year-old Tina Schofield while the best man congratulates the blushing bride.

Whether Malcolm Allison was being his usual bullish self or whether he really believed his own words, his statement to the press that City would "terrify Europe" would come back to haunt him all too quickly. As champions of England, the Blues entered European competition for the first time and were given a tough draw against Turkish champions Fenerbahce. With no experience of continental football to draw upon, City were out-thought tactically at Maine Road and the game ended 0-0.

Two weeks later and the dubious pleasure of European competition hit Mercer's men full in the face. Despite taking the lead through Tony Coleman, City lost 2-1 and were out at the first hurdle. Inexperience plus a difficult baptism in the competition conspired towards an early exit and the domestic scene was once again the focus for the club. But the champions were finding the defence of their title difficult and by late November they had won only four of their opening 19 League games. Floundering near the bottom of the table, the Blues only briefly showed glimpses of the form that had won them the Division One crown the season before.

The goals had dried up somewhat and only now and then – particularly at Maine Road – did City click into gear, with successive home wins against West Brom (5-1), Burnley (7-0) and Chelsea (4-1). So wretched was the club's away

As City's hopes of a successful title defence faded, the players were left to pick up more than just shattered dreams after a bottle smashed into the Blues' penalty area away to Tottenham. Today, the players would probably be asked to leave the pitch, but 40 years ago it was the players themselves who made the pitch safe to play on again.

form that they would win only twice on the road all season – at Sunderland and Manchester United. The final stats at home were only slightly worse than the previous campaign, but their away form resembled that of a side destined for Division Two. City's annoying inconsistency was once again haunting their ambitions.

No doubt the loss of skipper Tony Book was proving a devastating blow to the Blues, but he made a miraculous recovery from a serious Achilles tendon injury to once again lead the side in the New Year.

It was left to the FA Cup to provide the relief of a frustrating period for the club as they steamrollered towards the final with a determination and focus that had been absent from their League performances. Luton, Newcastle and Blackburn were dispatched along the way and single goal victories against Spurs and Everton set up a final against Leicester City where a glorious Neil Young strike won the trophy for City. A fitting end to an up-and-down season and Book was named joint Player of the Year by his fellow professionals for both his recovery and leadership during the second half of the campaign.

Wembley-bound Blues

24th April 1969: City players leave Piccadilly Station bound for Wembley and an FA Cup final with Leicester City.

Young at Heart!

Neil Young smashes home the winner against Leicester City to bring the FA Cup back to Maine Road. It was the fourth time the Blues had lifted the trophy and the first triumph for 13 years.

Thousands line the streets as the FA Cup winners return to Manchester. It was City's second major trophy inside 12 months and it seemed Europe was next for the all-conquering Blues.

"We've won the Cup!" Malcolm Allison leads the singing outside the Town Hall.

ABOVE: Running, running, running – City trained hard and played hard. Wythenshawe Park was a regular base for the Blues, though Tony Coleman (far right doesn't look overly impressed.

LEFT: June 1969: Mike Summerbee does special training with ex-Great Britain miler Stan Taylor at Longford Park Athletic track under the direction of Joe Lancaster, as Malcolm Allison attempts to take his team to the next level of fitness. A disappointing League campaign had seen the defending champions finish 13th and despite winning the FA Cup, Mercer and Allison expected more from their players.

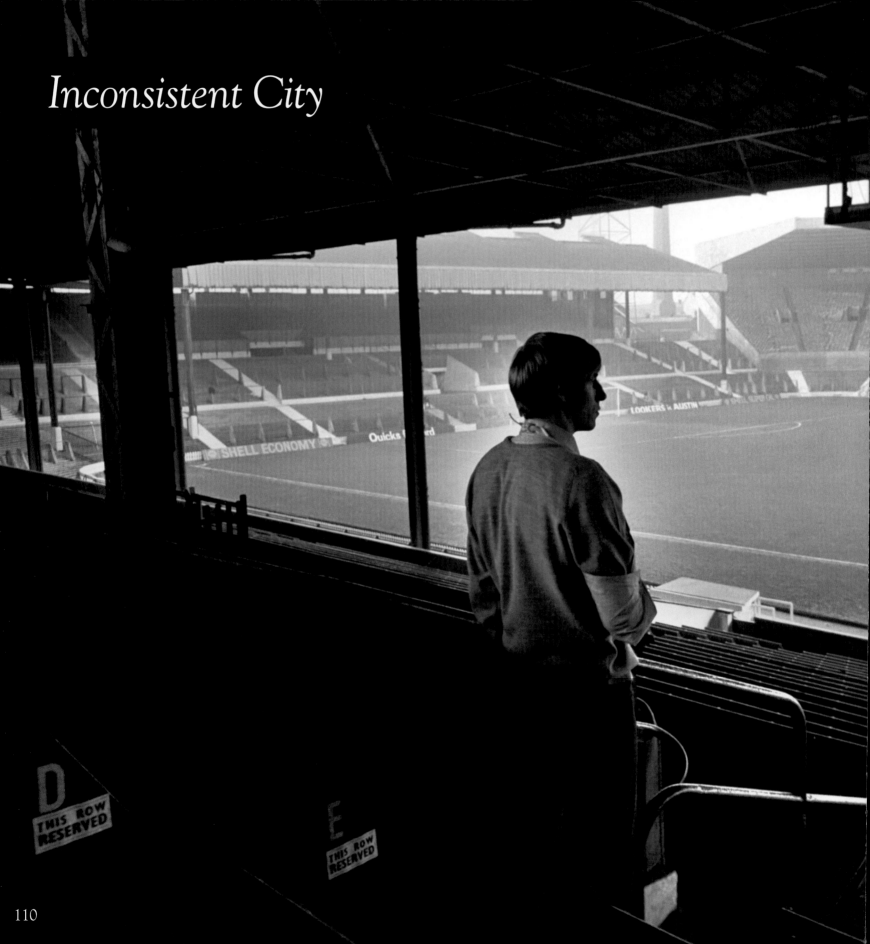

Inconsistent City

LEFT: A shoulder injury keeps Colin Bell out of the crucial League Cup semi-final second leg. Bell surveys Old Trafford and wonders how his team will fare without him – he needn't have worried as a late equalizer from Mike Summerbee sent City back to Wembley with a 2-2 draw giving the Blues a 4-3 aggregate victory.

BELOW: Despite having largely the same players throughout the 1968/9 and 1969/70 campaigns, City showed only flashes of the brilliance that had made them League champions. This 4-0 win at West Ham was all too rare as the Blues instead became more of a Cup team with another Wembley final on the horizon. Perhaps the Cup exploits took something from the League form and the chance to dominate English football slowly began to slip away.

–LEGENDS–

Joe Corrigan

For many, during the 1970s Joe Corrigan *was* Manchester City. Signed in 1966, Corrigan was third-choice keeper behind Ken Mulhearn and Harry Dowd during the late 1960s. He was given his chance towards the end of the 1968/9 season and became the No.1 in the following season , but his confidence suffered and weight soared as the fans began to lose confidence in his ability.

Malcolm Allison was determined Corrigan would make the grade and prove his judgement to be correct and he spent hours practising with the giant keeper long after the other players had left. Despite a number of high-profile faux pas during his early years, Corrigan held onto his place for the next four seasons and never made less than 30 starts in the League before City signed Motherwell's Keith MacRae to challenge for the No.1 jersey.

For the next two years Joe was playing second fiddle to MacRae, but after the Scot was injured during a 1-0 defeat at Leicester, Corrigan was reinstated. Having worked tirelessly in training, he had lost a great deal of weight and looked slimmer and fitter than ever before. The steely determination showed through in his performances and he missed just one of the next 223 League matches in an incredible run of appearances stretching more than seven years.

Despite his achievements, Joe was the third-choice England keeper, with a succession of national bosses preferring Peter Shilton and Ray Clemence – both excellent keepers in their own right. Had Corrigan played at almost any other period since, he would have been England's No.1 for perhaps a decade.

After more than 600 games for City, he played his last match for the club in a 4-1 defeat to Swansea at the Vetch Field. It was a disappointing note on which to leave the Blues as he headed to America for pastures new. City were relegated two months after Joe's departure.

Joe Corrigan trains long and hard after everyone else has showered and gone. Malcolm Allison was convinced Corrigan could be one of the game's greats and it was he, more often than not, who would push the future England keeper to the limit.

FOOTBALL
-STATS-

Joe Corrigan

Name: Joe Corrigan

Born: 1948

Signed: 1966, Sale FC

Playing career: 1967–84

Clubs: Manchester City, Seattle, Brighton, Stoke, Norwich

City appearances: 602 (+ 1 as a substitute)

Goals: 0

Dog's Life for Derek?

City youth-team graduate Derek Jeffries takes his dog Blackie for a run in a park near his home in Longsight. Jeffries played only 93 times for the Blues during a seven-year period before leaving for Crystal Palace in 1973.

You Play With The Wrong Shaped Ball. Mate!

World in union – City boss Joe Mercer meets South Africa rugby union team boss Corrie Bornman, of the Springboks, and Joe Mercer during a visit to Manchester.

Can You Spot Bobby Moore?

City players take a tour of Bobby Moore's
suede-and-leather factory on a visit to London.

Mid-table Blues

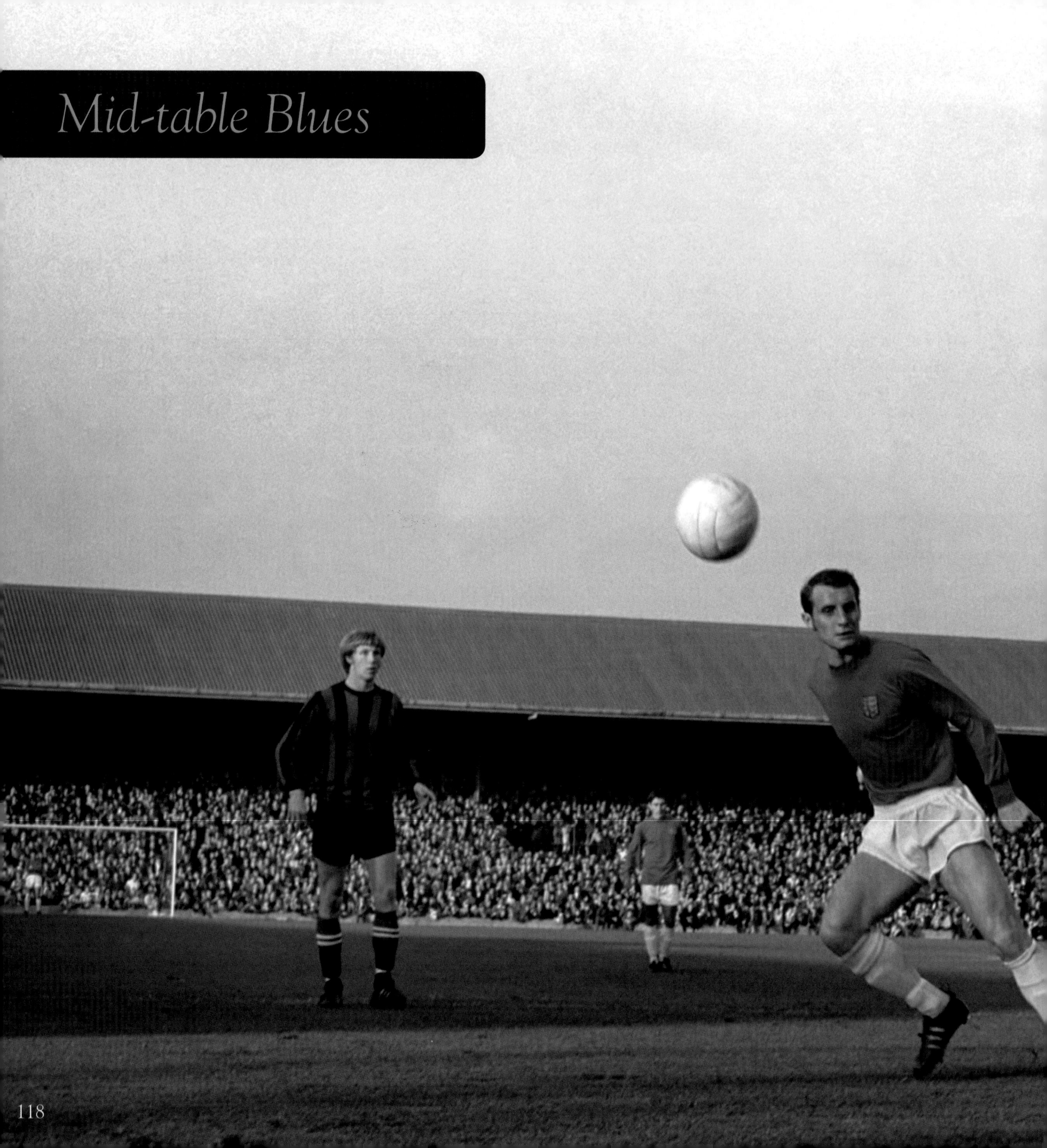

City take on Ipswich at Portman Road in a First Division clash that ended 1-1. The Blues were brilliant one week, average the next, in a frustrating season in the League during which they never looked like defending their title successfully.

–LEGENDS–

Colin Bell

Malcolm Allison knew a thoroughbred when he saw one and after convincing the City board to part with £60,000, he bought the Bury midfielder, Colin Bell. Allison put him straight into the Blues' midfield and Bell slotted in as if he had always been there, helping his new club to the Second Division title a couple of months after his arrival.

Within two years, City had won the First Division title with Bell who was inspirational throughout the campaign. The fans loved his driving style and seemingly limitless stamina. He was the beating heart of the team and he helped inspire the club to as yet uncharted heights. Bell won his first England cap in 1968 – the first of 48, which is still a club record. While Summerbee, Lee and Doyle would wind-up the opposition, the press and opposing fans, Bell quietly ticked along in the background, painfully shy, preferring to let his feet do the talking to great effect.

Nicknamed "The King of the Kippax", he was to Manchester City what George Best was to Manchester United. As the years went by, Bell's influence seemed to grow stronger rather than fade – while many believe Rodney Marsh's signing cost City the 1971/2 League title, few noted that Colin Bell had missed nine games through injury and the Blues won just four of those matches in his absence. A terrible tackle by Martin Buchan in 1975 and another by Ray Kennedy later in the season ensured Bell was sidelined for the next 18 months.

Quietly and stoically, he continued the long, painful road back to some kind of fitness, pounding the streets around Maine Road, and as some mobility returned to his knee he began training again. His comeback as a second-half sub against Newcastle on Boxing Day 1977 saw one of the most emotional ovations ever witnessed at Maine Road, but he soldiered on, if a shadow of his former self. Finally, the pain and heartache of never being able to move fluidly on a pitch again forced his inevitable retirement. It is unlikely City will ever have a player quite as complete as Colin Bell again.

FOOTBALL
–STATS–

Colin Bell

Name: Colin Bell

Born: 1946

Signed: 1966, Bury

Playing career: 1963–80

Clubs: Bury, Manchester City, San Jose

City appearances: 489 (+ 3 as a substitute)

Goals: 152

AGENTS WANTED
FOR
MANCHESTER CITY DEVELOPMENT

CITY BINGO

Room for Improvement

As the decade drew to a close, one thing in need of redevelopment was Maine Road. Almost 50 years old, the last uncovered terrace – the North Stand – was turned into a new all-seater stand with a roof and electronic scoreboard.

The world at his feet – a pensive Malcolm Allison, 1970.

Francis Lee blasts the ball past Leeds United's Gary Sprake. The Blues lost 2-1, but Lee's reputation as one of the country's leading strikers continued to grow with

Room For Another, Skip?

The trophy cabinet was about to get two more pieces of silverware with the 1969/70 campaign ending with a double triumph both at home and in Europe. Here, Tony Book and Ian Bowyer share a joke among the replica cups already won – except for the World Cup on the far left, though Malcolm Allison did once claim his team would be the first side to play on the moon.

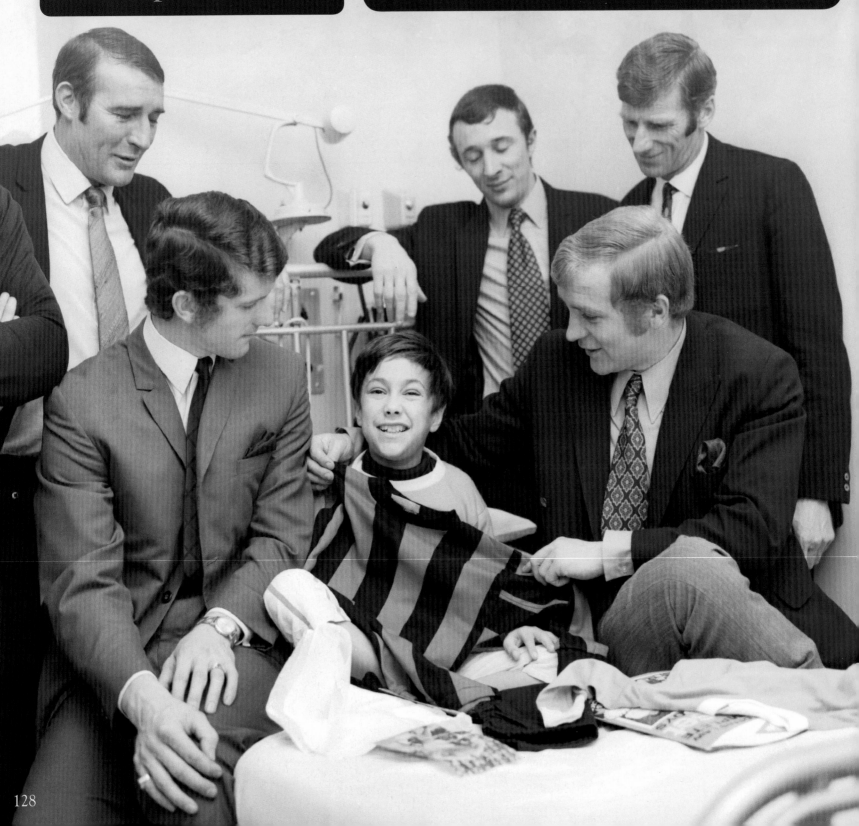

A Surprise Visit!

The players pay a visit to a young City fan awaiting a kidney transplant shortly before Christmas. Player visits were not uncommon, particularly around the festive season.

Let's be Frank!

Altrincham forward Frank Carrodus collects his boots at Moss Lane for the final time before signing for City – the Blues recruited from non-League and the lower divisions on a regular basis, always keeping well within the budgets. With no TV money, little income from sponsorships and not even a sniff of a wealthy owner among the 92 League contenders, clubs were run on the income received at the gate alone.

City skipper Tony Book keeps a close eye on future team-mate Joe Royle during a clash with Everton at Maine Road. This game ended in a 1-1 draw.

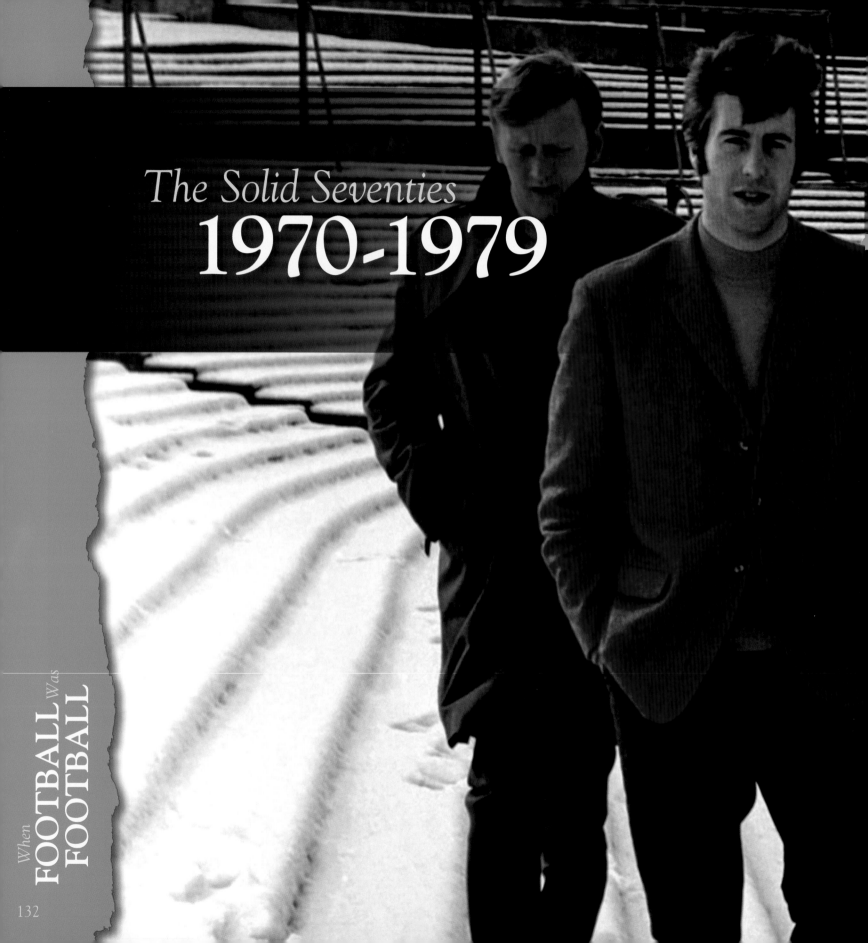

The Solid Seventies
1970-1979

Following an exhausting trip back to England after a 0-0 midweek Cup Winners' Cup quarter-final draw with Academica Coimbra in Portugal, Tony Book and Ken Mulhearn join club physio Peter Blakey for treatment at Arsenal's Highbury. The snow that delayed the team's return to London is still evident on the North Bank terrace and the League Cup final itself is in doubt thanks to the unusually cold spring weather.

1970 City win League Cup with a 2-1 victory over West Brom. City win first European trophy after beating Górnik Zabrze 2-1 in Vienna. 1972 Rodney Marsh signs for a club record £200,000. After leading the table with just a couple of games to go, City finish fourth in the table, a point behind champions Derby County. Joe Mercer leaves City to join Coventry. Malcolm Allison becomes City's new manager. 1973 Johnny Hart takes over from Allison, but ill-health means Ron Saunders is named as new boss. Denis Law returns to City after being freed by Manchester United. 1974 City lose League Cup final to Wolves. Saunders is sacked; Tony Book takes charge and oversees win over United that relegates Reds. 1976 City win League Cup with 2-1 win over Newcastle. 1977 City finish runners-up in League to Liverpool. 1978 City finish fourth in League. 1979 Malcolm Allison returns to City as head coach.

IT'S A BOY! Yet more celebrations for Neil Young as he learns he has become a father a few days before the 1970 League Cup final. Keeper Ken Mulhearn enjoys a glass of champagne, though neither player would feature in the final itself.

Franny Lee fires home another successful penalty –
No. 4 Mike Doyle can't bear to watch.

The League Cup 1970

As City moved into a new decade, the League was again the poor relation to cup competitions and though City crashed out as holders of the FA Cup to United in the fourth round, the League Cup and European Cup Winners' Cup would prove an entirely different matter. With the lessons of Fenerbahce learned in the European Cup, City entered the Cup Winners' Cup with a steely determination to prove coach Malcolm Allison had been right to say his men would "terrify Europe".

A fantastic 3-3 draw away to Athletic Bilbao was followed by an equally impressive 3-0 home victory. In the League Cup, City had dispatched Southport and Liverpool. The two competitions would run in tandem all season. By November, City had seen off Everton and QPR to line up a tasty two-legged semi-final with United. It was to be a painful season for the Reds in derby games as City thrashed them 4-0 in the League in November with Colin Bell grabbing a brace. Belgian side SK Lierse were dumped out 8-0 on aggregate in the European Cup Winners' Cup , leaving the Blues to look forward to further action the following spring.

In the League Cup, the Blues beat United 2-1 at Maine Road and two weeks later City booked an immediate return to Wembley with a 2-2 draw at Old Trafford in the return leg.

Joe Mercer described the Wembley surface for the final as "a pig of a pitch" following the Horse of the Year Show days earlier. In a gruelling game, Glyn Pardoe hit an extra-time winner for City after Mike Doyle had levelled Jeff Astle's early strike for West Brom. The League Cup had become the third major trophy Tony Book had lifted in just under three years – an incredible achievement – and there was more to come.

March 1970: Joe Corrigan takes an injured Arthur Mann off while Tommy Booth allows himself a wry smile in the foreground – the pitch resembles a cabbage patch.

> " *I've never seen a football pitch like it – it was a pig of a pitch.*
>
> Joe Mercer "

Look What We've Got!

The City players parade the trophy to their fans on a lap of honour after the match. The lucky red-and-black-striped kit had done the trick again. From left to right: Arthur Mann, Francis Lee, Joe Corrigan and George Heslop.

–LEGENDS–

Mike Doyle

A boyhood City fan, Mike Doyle would go on to be one of the best players in the club's history – he was certainly one of the most committed. In fact, there were many reasons why Doyle was idolized by the City fans, but his very public hatred of Manchester United struck a particularly pleasing chord with the supporters. Doyle didn't just hate the Reds, he loathed them with a passion and throughout his career he always found that little bit extra when the Manchester derby came around. An intelligent player, able to burst forward from the back with the ball, Doyle became an integral part of Mercer and Allison's team in the late 1960s. He missed only a dozen games between August 1967 and May 1971 and of those City lost nine and drew the other three.

He played in every major final during the Blues' glory years and scored a vital equalizer in the 1970 League Cup final, as well as a crucial strike in the European Cup Winners' Cup semi-final against Schalke 04 at Maine Road. Doyle would probably have gone to Mexico in 1970 had his wife not been ill in hospital and had he not told Sir Alf Ramsey he was unavailable – he won only six caps for his country and perhaps should have won many more. Despite being a natural leader, it wasn't until 1975 that he finally won the captain's armband, forging a fantastic centre-half partnership with Dave Watson. There was no prouder man than Doyle when he lifted the League Cup in 1976. He very nearly skippered his team to the League title the following season, just missing out to Liverpool by one point. He joined Stoke in 1978, having made more than 500 appearances over a 16-year period at City.

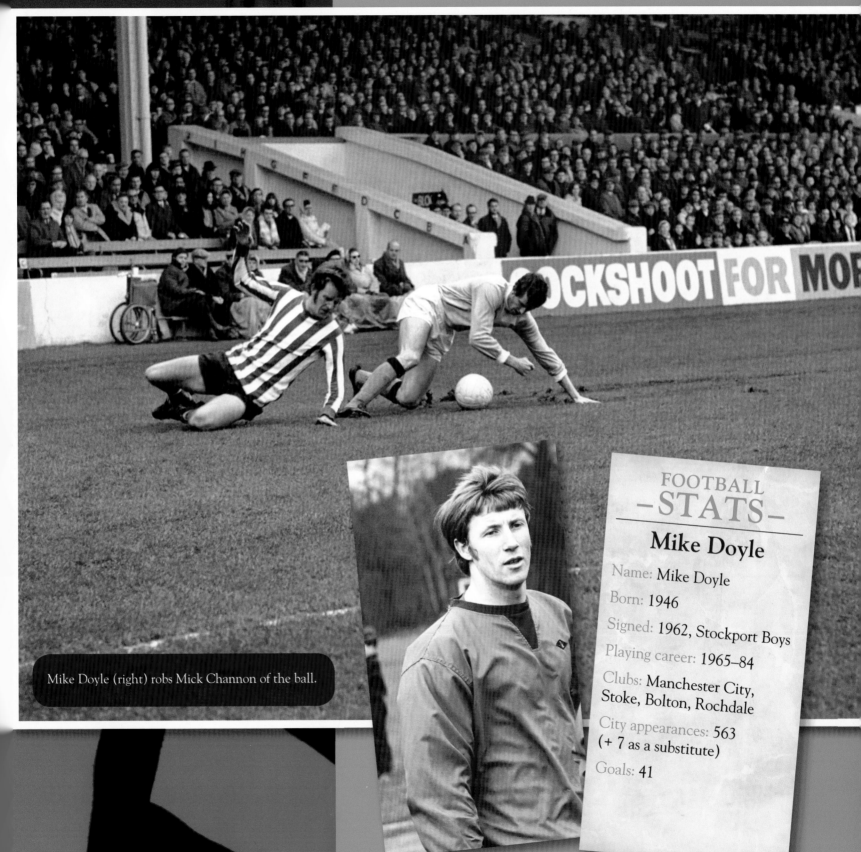

Mike Doyle (right) robs Mick Channon of the ball.

FOOTBALL
–STATS–

Mike Doyle

Name: Mike Doyle

Born: 1946

Signed: 1962, Stockport Boys

Playing career: 1965–84

Clubs: Manchester City, Stoke, Bolton, Rochdale

City appearances: 563 (+ 7 as a substitute)

Goals: 41

...were paired with Portuguese outfit Académica Coimbra for the quarter... of the European Cup Winners' Cup and played out a bruising 0-0 draw ...in the first leg with Tony Towers scoring the only goal of the return leg ...the Blues into the semi-final.

...man side Schalke 04 were the only obstacle standing between City and ...European final and won the first leg 1-0, but the Blues were awesome ...return, winning 5-1 in front of an ecstatic Maine Road. They would ...avel to Austria to face Polish side Gornik Zabrze in the final.

...Blues had finished in 10th place in Division One by the time they ...out on a rain-sodden Vienna evening. With the majority of the 8,000 ...om Manchester uncovered, City set about the Poles and Neil Young ...nny Lee scored the goals in a memorable 2-1 win. Tony Book again ...nother major trophy and Allison later claimed he had been right all ...bout his side dominating Europe, but had just got it a year wrong! ...ile, the City fans kept pinching themselves to believe it was all ...appening.

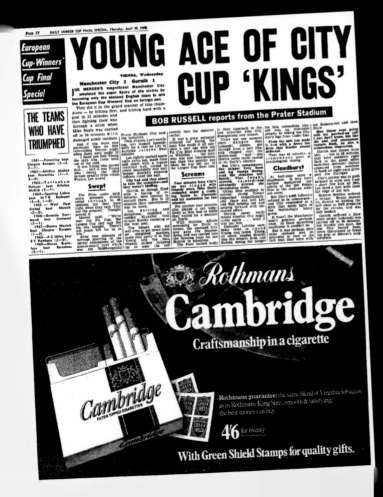

A new decade, another trophy. A drenched City win the 1970 European Cup Winners' Cup final in Vienna against Gornik Zabrze, with goals from Franny Lee and Neil Young. Captain Tony Book is once again held aloft by his team-mates as his own personal fairytale continued.

Kings of the City: a jubilant Joe Mercer joins in the Cup Winners' Cup celebrations on the homecoming tour of Manchester.

Neil Young, captured forever in this fantastic image of his goal against Gornik.

That's a Weight Off!

RIGHT: July, 1971: Joe Corrigan accepts the offer from the *Daily Mirror* to prove he isn't carrying excess weight as he comes under fire from a number of City supporters. Some of Joe's early years were dogged with high-profile gaffes, but he would knuckle down and go on to become a club legend.

Denis Law, enjoying his second spell with the Blues during a 1973 clash with Spurs at White Hart Lane.

Tough Going...

The Blues finished the 1970/1 season with no silverware to show for their efforts. An 11th-placed finish in the League and little success in either domestic cup competition, City's only hope of continuing the silver streak was in the European Cup Winners' Cup, but despite reaching the semi-final, an injury-hit side lost the first leg to Chelsea 1-0 and the second leg went the same way, with the Pensioners winning by a solitary goal – there was to be no addition to the burgeoning trophy cabinet this season.

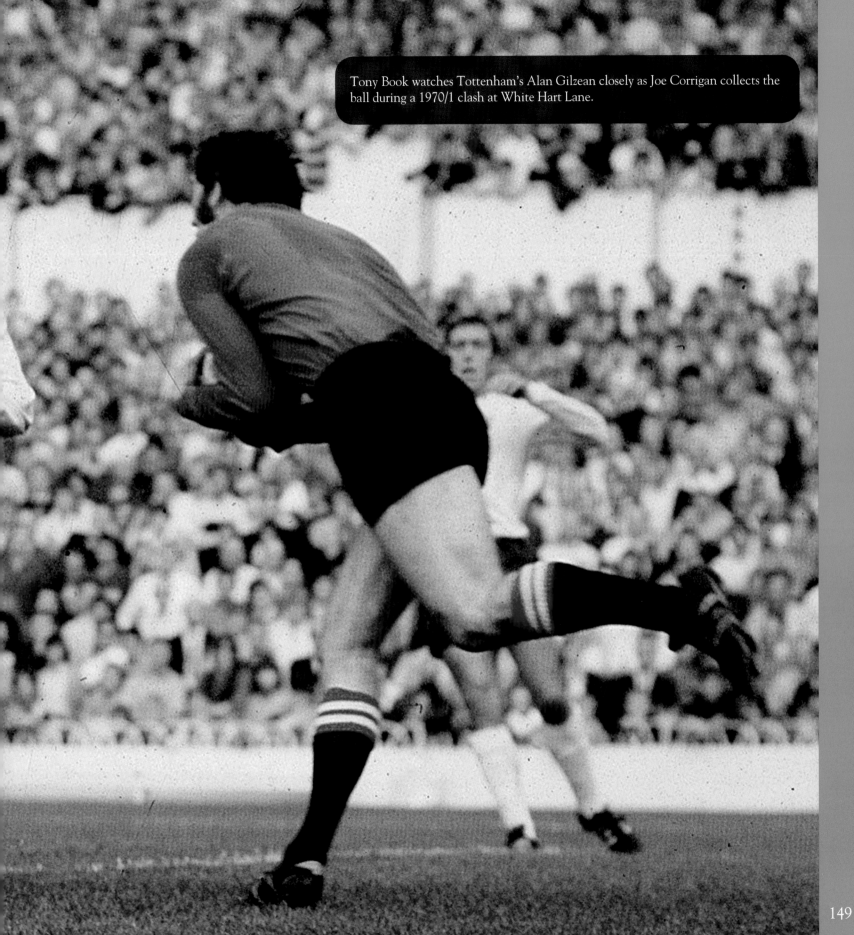

Tony Book watches Tottenham's Alan Gilzean closely as Joe Corrigan collects the ball during a 1970/1 clash at White Hart Lane.

Tony Book

Tony Book's story is, in many ways a fairytale. After spending most of his career with non-League Bath City, Malcolm Allison took him to Plymouth aged 30 and when Allison left to coach City he again took the dependable Book with him. His signing raised one or two eyebrows, it's fair to say. Book was 32 and had never played in the top division, but Allison persisted and an initially reluctant Joe Mercer was forced to concede that he himself hadn't signed for Arsenal until he had turned 31. City paid Plymouth £17,000 and from there on, things just got better and better for the former Bath brickie.

Book was soon made captain and his first campaign as skipper saw City crowned Division One champions, though that was just the beginning of the club's most glorious period in their history.

Book missed the first half of the 1968/9 season with an Achilles injury, but recovered to lift the FA Cup and was then named PFA Player of the Year, an award he shared with Dave Mackay. In his third campaign he lifted the League Cup and the European Cup Winners' Cup within the space of six unforgettable weeks – his fourth trophy in three years as captain – not bad for a 35-year-old in only his fifth season in League football. He continued playing until he retired during the 1973/4 season. After Johnny Hart and Ron Saunders' brief reign as managers, a player's committee demanded Book be installed as manager – one of his first tasks was to oversee the 1-0 win at Old Trafford that condemned Manchester United to the Second Division.

He had the total respect of the supporters, players and board, and his fellow professionals thought he was a bit special, too. George Best once declared Book was his most difficult opponent – quite an accolade. He went on to manage the club with great dignity and turned an ageing side heading in the wrong direction into a genuine force again, as well as lifting the League Cup in 1976.

Tony with the League Cup trophy in 1970.

FOOTBALL
–STATS–

Tony Book

Name: Tony Book

Born: 1943

Signed: 1966, Plymouth Argyle

Playing career: 1955–74

Clubs: Frome Town, Bath City, Plymouth, Manchester City

City appearances: 306 (+ 3 as a substitute)

Goals: 3

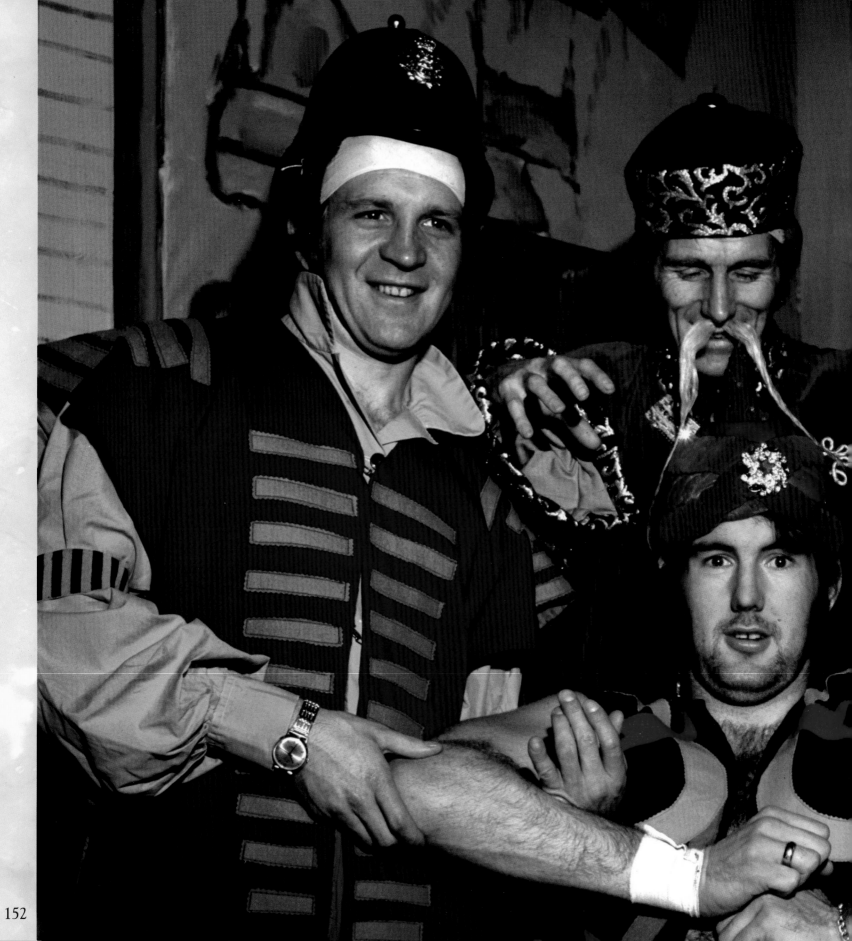

Oh Yes
They Are!

LEFT: The Manchester City
panto was a great tradition,
with the players regularly taking
part in the Christmas fun at
the City Social Club. Franny
Lee and Mike Summerbee flank
Joe Corrigan, while a fiendish
Tony Book hovers over.

Style over Substance?

Despite the rumblings behind the scenes, Joe Mercer was still the manager of City for the beginning of the 1971/2 season. By October, Malcolm Allison was effectively in charge, with Mercer becoming general manager.

On the pitch the Blues were doing well, with only two defeats in their opening 19 fixtures. Franny Lee was making the headlines for his success from the penalty spot and often won the kicks himself with what many considered a perfected dive. Lee shrugged off accusations and continued to score with or without the aid of penalties.

November saw a fantastic Manchester derby watched by more than 63,000 fans at Maine Road with Mike Summerbee scoring at the death to earn his side a share of the spoils in a thrilling 3-3 draw. Wyn Davies was now leading the line for the Blues and many believed they were on their way to another League title.

Behind the scenes, Joe Mercer was becoming more and more disillusioned with his treatment by the City board. He was being dealt with shabbily by the chairman and directors and felt – quite rightly – he deserved more respect. The problem would not go away and continued throughout the season.

By the middle of March, City were four points clear at the top of the table and seemingly heading for the title. For the final push, Allison signed Rodney Marsh for a club record fee of £200,000 – he felt the maverick forward would be the icing on the cake to the side. However, accommodating such a talent meant a change of style for the team who managed just four wins from the final nine.

City finished fourth and many blamed the arrival of Marsh for the disappointing finish. There was no doubt his style of play meant slower build-ups where City's strength had previously been quick counter-attacking football. Nobody will ever know if it was the reason or whether it was simply a dip in form at the wrong time. At least Franny Lee set a new record for penalties scored in a season – 15 – to add to his impressive tally of 33.

In June 1972 Joe Mercer left Maine Road to become general manager at Coventry City, leaving the majority of fans disgusted at the club's handling of a man who had made their side one of the best in Europe for several years. What could have ended a memorable season had ended with bitter disappointment all round.

Record £200,000 signing Marsh ensures a full house for the crucial visit of Chelsea. The 1-0 keeps the Blues on course for the title, but just one draw out of the next three games sees Der Leeds and Liverpool gain valuable ground – m blame the arrival of Marsh for disrupting the t fast-flowing football. Whether or not Marsh w the reason City didn't go on to lift the title, h can't be held solely responsible for the failure. eventually finished fourth in 1971/2 in one of closest finishes to a League campaign ever.

March 1972: New-signing Rodney Marsh surveys
the terraces where he will soon become an idol.

Return of the Lawman

Denis Law returns for his second spell at City.

And Denis has done it.

Gerald Sinstadt

With Malcolm Allison quitting halfway through a dismal 1972/3 campaign, Johnny Hart took the reins and was still at the helm for the 1973/4 season, but few believed he could survive the cut-throat world of football management or fill the cavernous void left by Allison. It was Hart, though, who pulled off a major coup in signing United legend Denis Law on a free transfer during the close season. There was much surprise at the deal, particularly among the Old Trafford faithful who were understandably concerned at losing Law to their neighbours.

The former Scotland captain – who would come back to haunt the Reds later in the season – made his second debut for the Blues against Birmingham City and scored two goals in a 3-1 win. The City team was in a transitional period with an ageing line-up and several players coming to the end of their careers. One of them, Tony Book, was now 38 years old and had given the club magnificent service since signing from Plymouth, but time had finally caught up with the most successful captain ever at Maine Road.

In the boardroom, Peter Swales became chairman in October and immediately began looking for a replacement for the ailing Hart who was suffering debilitating illness that made it impossible for him to continue. Though the general consensus among the players was to promote Book, Swales employed dour disciplinarian Ron Saunders, boss of Norwich City. The League form was decidedly average, but Saunders did guide his new club to the 1974 League Cup final only to be beaten 2-1 by Wolves after a mammoth 11-game journey to Wembley. Dennis Tueart arrived from Sunderland shortly after as Saunders sought to add firepower to his shot-shy team, but with fans and players unhappy with the Saunders' methods, Swales sacked him over Easter.

Tony Book was given the chance to show he was just as good a leader off the pitch as he had been on it and all seemed well again at Maine Road. The Blues went into the last game of the season against United safe, but the Reds needed a victory to have any chance of survival. Almost 57,000 were in Old Trafford when with minutes left the unthinkable happened. With the scores deadlocked at 0-0, the ball came to Law inside the box and he back-heeled it past Alex Stepney into the net to confirm United's demise – though they would have gone down whatever the score due to results elsewhere, not that City fans cared.

27th April 1974: Denis Law's back-heel condemns Manchester United to the Second Division and sparks a crowd invasion.

3rd March 1974: City lose the League Cup final 2-1 to Wolverhampton Wanderers after a patchy display. Colin Bell scored for the Blues who were skippered by Mike Summerbee.

For Whom the Bell Tolls

Colin Bell prepares for his canoe race during the 1974 series of Superstars. Bell and the rest of the England team were able to commit to extraneous projects following the failure to qualify for the 1974 World Cup.

BELOW: One of Bell's favourite images, taken during the 1970 World Cup in Mexico as England took on West Germany – and no, we didn't win that one, either!

Prior to the 2010/11 season, this was City's last victory away to Arsenal. Goals from Asa Hartford, Rodney Marsh and Joe Royle helped the Blues to a 3-2 victory at Highbury. Willie Donachie is pictured in the thick of the action.

Rebirth of the Blues

The 1974/5 season saw several changes in personnel as Book moulded the side into his image. Francis Lee was transferred to Derby County, Asa Hartford arrived from West Brom and the Blues began once again to look like a strong, settled side. They would end in eighth position and repeated the feat for the 1975/6 campaign, by which time Joe Royle and Dave Watson had been added to the squad and Mike Summerbee had departed. Rodney Marsh was transferred to Tampa Bay Rowdies amid much controversy and Colin Bell had been lost to a crippling knee injury in a League Cup tie against United, but the Blues went on to win the competition trophy with a wonder goal from Tueart against Newcastle United.

City celebrate victory over Chelsea, April 1975.

The maverick Rodney Marsh who delighted and frustrated in equal measure. Every bit the rock-and-roll footballer, he is pictured here shortly before his falling out with manager Tony Book.

Cup Kings – Again!

RIGHT: One of the most famous Wembley goals ever scored: Dennis Tueart's spectacular overhead kick wins the 1976 League Cup final and Tony Book's first trophy as City manager.

BELOW: 28th February 1976: Teenage winger Peter Barnes bursts through a four-man wall of Newcastle defenders to score the first goal of the League Cup final.

169

So Close, Yet So Far Away

There were more new arrivals for the 1976/7 campaign, with Brian Kidd and Jimmy Conway joining Book's side and long-serving defender Alan Oakes leaving the club after 18 years at Maine Road. Paul Power was yet another promising youngster who was making a name for himself as City prepared an all-out assault on the League title. The Blues began with only two defeats in their first 25 games with Joe Corrigan and his defenders keeping 13 clean sheets. UEFA Cup interest had ended in the first round against Juventus and Aston Villa and Leeds had been responsible for domestic departures from cup competitions. With only the League to concentrate on, it was Liverpool and the Blues neck-and-neck on the run-in. City suffered a few crushing blows. United completed the double over Book's men at Old Trafford and in April Liverpool beat City 2-1 at Anfield. Worse was to come as Derby thrashed City 4-0 and both Villa and Everton took a point off them in the crucial run-in. By the end, Liverpool had won the League by a point and the Blues were left to rue missed opportunities during an excellent League programme.

Southampton and England striker Mike Channon was the only notable close-season purchase for the start of 1977/8. City were again consistent, but were again knocked out of the UEFA Cup at the first hurdle. Dennis Tueart had scored three hat-tricks by the time Newcastle were sent packing 4-0 on Boxing Day – the day Colin Bell made an emotional return to first-team football after an agonising fight to save his career. The win over the Geordies was the first of seven successive League victories, keeping the pressure on Brian Clough's Nottingham Forest, but the gap would never be closed and City – now without a New York Cosmos-bound Tueart – finished in fourth. It was to be the last assault on the title for many years.

LEFT: Dennis Tueart wheels away after putting City 2-0 up at Elland Road in the FA Cup fourth round and Colin Bell celebrates. With 10 minutes remaining, the Leeds fans invaded the pitch in an attempt to get the match abandoned. When the game was restarted, Leeds pulled one back, but the Blues held on for an impressive win.

End of an Era

November 1978: Colin Bell at home with his wife Marcie, daughter Dawn and new-born son Jon. Bell's valiant attempt to beat a knee injury sustained against Manchester United in 1975 ultimately failed, though he did manage to play a number of games before officially retiring. A half-fit Bell was still worth two of most other players in the eyes of City fans.

How City could have used a fully-fit Colin Bell as they agonisingly finished a point behind Liverpool in 1976/77 – above, Ray Clemence chases a Mike Doyle shot that trickled just past the post as the Kippax holds its collective breath.

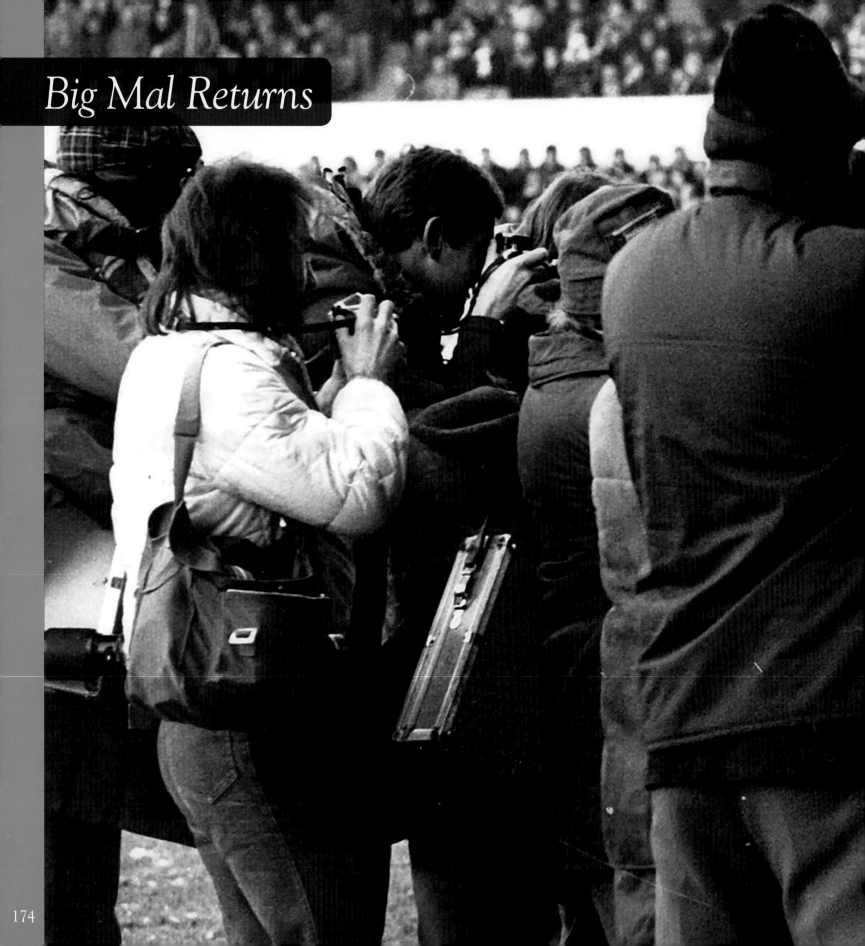

January 1979: Malcolm Allison returns as City's first-team coach waving to photographers prior to the 1-1 draw with Leeds.

A Series of Unfortunate Events

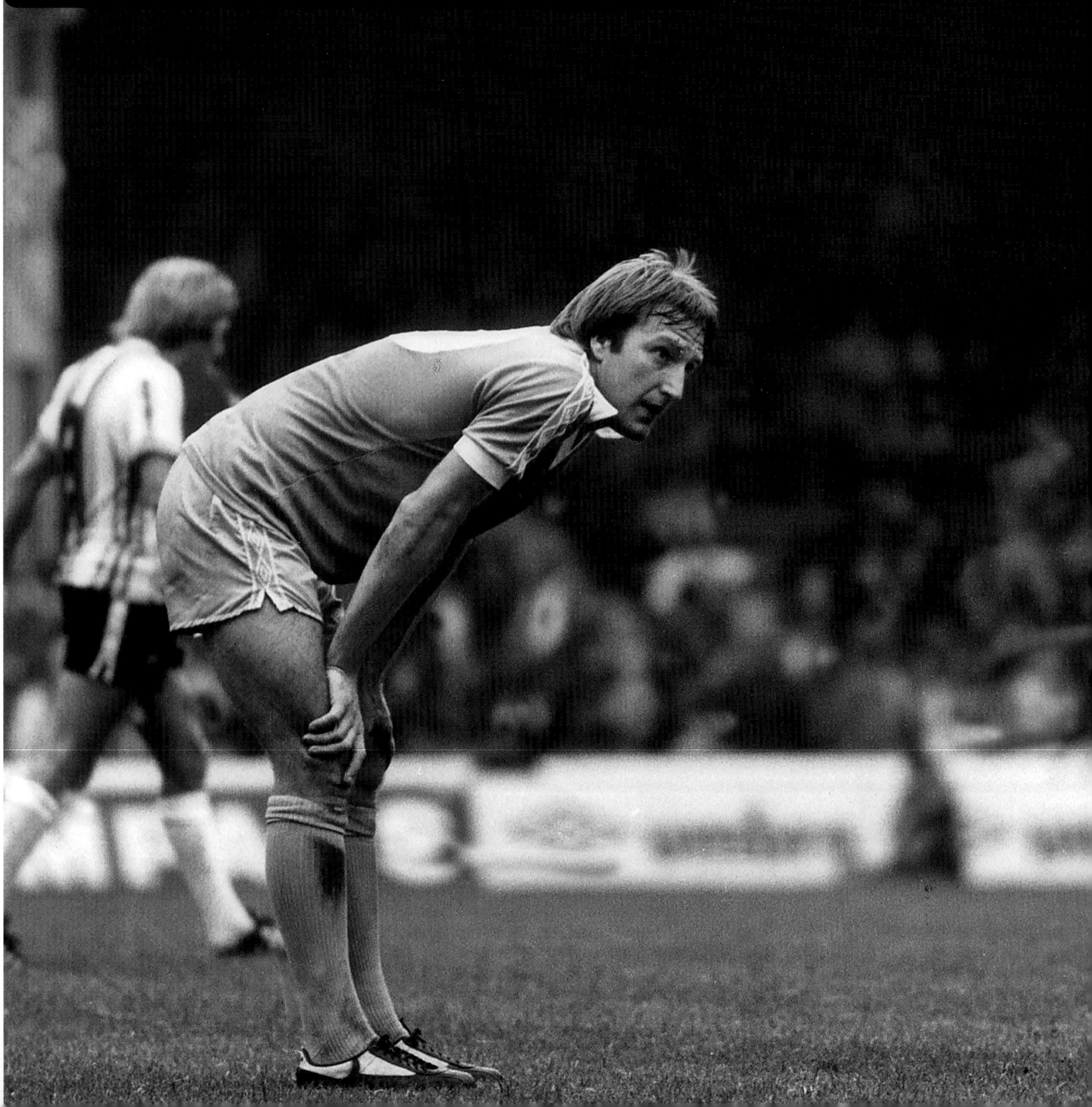

The highlight of a largely disappointing 1978/9 season was the arrival of Polish World Cup captain Kaziu Deyna and a terrific run in the UEFA Cup. City beat FC Twente and Standard Liège to win a plum tie with Italian giants AC Milan. The first game in Italy was postponed due to fog and rearranged for the following afternoon. The Blues raced into a 2-0 lead with Paul Power scoring an amazing solo goal, but the tie ended 2-2. The second leg found the Blues in imperious form and goals from Kidd, Booth and Hartford gave them a 3-0 lead at the break. There were no more goals and City headed into the quarter-finals to face German outfit Borussia Monchengladbach where they would lose 4-2 on aggregate.

Deyna showed only glimpses of the brilliance that had made him a legend in his homeland, but his skills were, on occasion, a joy to watch. Meanwhile, concerned at the Blues' dip in fortunes, Swales decided there was only one man who could help turn things around. By the start of 1979 Malcolm Allison was back at Maine Road as coach – a move that was warmly greeted by the City fans. Dennis Tueart returned from New York Cosmos two-thirds of the way through the programme, but a humiliating loss to Shrewsbury Town in the FA Cup and a finish of 15th – the club's lowest since 1967 – set alarm bells ringing.

It was the beginning of a devastating period for the club punctuated by incredible highs and soul-destroying lows. Kevin Reeves became the latest million-pound signing for the Blues, but his arrival altered little. Allison, now effectively in control of the team, guided City into the 1980s with a 1-0 defeat to Fourth Division Halifax Town. Mightily close to going down at one stage, City finished in 17th place with the side unrecognisable from just a year before. With the club in turmoil, chairman Swales began to wonder if bringing Big Mal back had been a huge mistake.

LEFT: The weight of pressure on Steve Daley is evident even during his first game in City colours. At £1,450,000, Daley became the most expensive player in the country and the expectations placed on him were simply too much. He was Malcolm Allison's marquee signing, but his signing swallowed up funds that could have rebuilt the successful 1970s team Allison had just dismantled. It was just one example of 18 months of madness that would take City the best part of 20 years to recover from.

Bouncing Back and Forth
1980-1994

Record-signing Steve Daley enjoys a rare happy moment in City colours as he scores during the 3-1 defeat at West Brom.

1980 Fourth Division Halifax knock City out of the FA Cup. Tony Book and Malcolm Allison sacked in October after City fail to win first 10 League games of 1980/1 season. John Bond becomes new City manager, signing Tommy Hutchison, Gerry Gow and Bobby McDonald for bargain fees. 1981 City lose 2-1 over two legs in the League Cup semi-final. City reach Centenary FA Cup final, but after drawing first game 1-1, lose replay 3-2. City sign Trevor Francis. 1982 City top the table after three games of the 1982/3 season. 1983 John Bond quits after City are beaten 4-0 by Brighton in the FA Cup. City relegated on final day of season following a late winner for Luton Town at Maine Road. Billy McNeill becomes City manager. 1985 City are promoted. 1987 City are relegated. 1988 City beat Huddersfield Town 10-1. 1989 City are promoted. City beat Manchester United 5-1. Mel Machin sacked and Howard Kendall becomes manager. 1990 Kendall quits and Peter Reid becomes boss. 1991 City finish fifth in Division One – the club's highest finish for 13 years – ahead of sixth-placed Manchester United. 1992 City finish fifth again. 1993 Brian Horton replaces the sacked Reid. 1994 The Kippax terraced stand is demolished and an all-seater stand built in its place.

Big Mal waves goodbye to the Kippax.

Swales Takes Action

The first full season of the 1980s would be unforgettable for City fans as the club – even by its own standards – went from one extreme to another. Big Mal was clinging on to his job for dear life and really should have been replaced in the summer, but such was his almost hypnotic hold on chairman Peter Swales and the board that he earned at least one more crack at revitalising the team.

It wasn't that Allison had lost his talent as a coach – the ability he had on the training ground could never diminish – it was more to do with the timing and lack of a Joe Mercer alongside him. Plus, the players from the late 1960s were a special bunch – the kind that only come along once in a blue moon. He was steering a sinking ship into deeper waters and signing players such as Steve Daley, Paul Sugrue and Barry Silkman proved ill judged – they simply weren't good enough. The first dozen games of the 1980/1 season were painful for all concerned and City fans had to endure some terrible matches before Swales did the decent thing and relieved Allison of his position.

The Name's Bond – John Bond

New boss John Bond takes his seat for the first time as City manager.

Malcolm Allison, perhaps the club's greatest coach and innovator, cuts a lonely figure on the bench as his Palace side are swept away.

Meanwhile, new boss John Bond sits in the stand as his team continue their amazing run of form since his arrival.

Every Dog Has Its Day...

Stray dogs were a common sight on matchdays at Maine Road during the early 1980s. This mutt, clearly a Red, ran the length of the pitch before cocking his leg up on the goal-post.

As the Blues waned towards the end of the 1970s, Joe Corrigan became ever more important to the club, almost single-handedly keeping opposition at bay on numerous occasions, though this shot from Frank Stapleton in the 1979 Manchester derby proved an exception.

On a Roll!

Just as he had done when he'd brought Ron Saunders to City, Peter Swales returned to Norwich City in search of a man big enough to save his club and build a brighter future. Enter John Bond; every bit the flamboyant larger-than-life character Swales felt was needed to erase the memory of a painful couple of years. Bond quit Carrow Road and headed north to take up the reigns of a club teetering on the brink.

The effect the new man had was nothing short of miraculous and undoubtedly his signing of three Scottish veterans for a total outlay of under £500,000 was one of the main reasons for the club's incredible turnaround. Gerry Gow was drafted from Bristol City and Bobby McDonald and Tommy Hutchison arrived from Coventry City. The trio were well respected within the game as good players, but none had set the world on fire with their previous sides. All that was about to change.

City began life under Bond with a closely fought battle with Birmingham City at Maine Road, where a last-minute Archie Gemmill penalty proved to be the only goal of the game. Bond was still in the process of bringing the three Scots to the club and again had to make do with what he already had for the visit of Spurs. He gave teenager Gary Buckley his debut, believing width was needed for his side, and City played with style to win their first game of the season 3-1.

From there on in, the Blues were a different team. They steadily climbed away from the foot of the table with a series of impressive wins and made progress in both cup competitions. For the League Cup, Bond's new signings were cup-tied so he was basically playing the same team Allison had been putting out before he was sacked and, for a while, it seemed as though there were two teams at Maine Road, both playing equally well. City reached the semi-final of the League Cup, but went out controversially to Liverpool 2-1 over two legs with at least one unbelievably bad refereeing decision robbing the Blues of a vital first-leg advantage.

In the FA Cup, there were a series of ironic pairings with Crystal Palace (Allison's new team) and then Norwich City (Bond's old team) in rounds three and four. Both were easily dispatched 4-0 and 6-0 respectively. A Tommy Booth header saw off the challenge of Fourth Division Peterborough at London Road and then City drew Everton in the last eight.

RIGHT: The Wembley trail continues with a 6-0 thumping of Norwich at Maine Road – sub Dave Bennett salutes the Kippax after putting the seal on a magnificent display, watched by 38,919 ecstatic fans.

Hamming It Up

March 1981: Never one to miss a photo opportunity, defender Tommy Booth hams it up for the camera as he receives his flu jab.

Kevin Bond and Joe Corrigan discuss a near miss for Ipswich Town in November 1981.

One Step Closer...

City travelled to Goodison Park, backed by more than 10,000 fans, and twice had to come from behind to earn a 2-2 draw. In front of 52,532 Maine Road fans, the Blues eased into the semi-finals thanks to two goals in a minute from full-back Bobby McDonald.

Up next were Bobby Robson's buoyant Ipswich Town at Villa Park. It was an unforgettable day for City fans as the Blues won 1-0 with a glorious Paul Power free kick in the 100th minute of the Centenary FA Cup competition. Many supporters would later say they enjoyed the semi-final even more than the final. Surely City's name was on the trophy – all the irony and victories against the odds suggested it must be.

RIGHT: Gerry Gow levels matters in the FA Cup quarter-final at Everton to help City earn a 2-2 draw. The Blues won the replay 3-1 at Maine Road.

The 1981 FA Cup Final

Thousands of City fans queued at Maine Road for hours for their Cup final tickets as excitement reached fever pitch in the blue half of Manchester, but there were nowhere near enough tickets to meet the demand. With a comfortable mid-table League position secured, the Blues walked out with Tottenham onto the lush Wembley turf for the 100th FA Cup final. The game ended 1-1 after Tommy Hutchison put City ahead and then bizarrely deflected a Hoddle free kick past Joe Corrigan for a late own goal. City still had chances to win the match in extra time but it wasn't to be.

The replay five days later was one of the most exciting the old stadium had ever witnessed and despite leading 2-1 with not much more than 15 minutes left, the Blues lost 3-2 after a wonderful solo goal from Argentinean Ricky Villa knocked the stuffing out of Bond's side. The dream was over and all the omens were proved wrong. It wasn't the storybook ending such a fairytale season had demanded.

ABOVE: City and Spurs meet the Queen Mother prior to the Centenary FA Cup final. Paul Power can be seen far right, but an ominous-looking Gerry Gow can be seen scowling over at the Spurs players.

RIGHT: A charged-up Tommy Hutchison, still smarting from the own goal he scored to bring Tottenham level, reacts angrily to a challenge by Garth Crooks.

The players salute the fans after a 1-1 draw with Spurs –
both goals scored by City's Tommy Hutchison.

193

Heartbreak as Villa Nicks It

> "
> As we drove away from Wembley on the team coach, Tommy Hutchison looked across at the stadium and said, 'I never want to see that place again.'
> "
>
> Joe Corrigan

Heartbreak as City concede a late goal in the epic 1981 FA Cup final replay against Spurs. Victory would have changed the club's fortunes in the 1980s, but the Ricky Villa winner was the beginning of a steady descent for the Blues who would take almost a decade to recover.

ABOVE: The much-loved, erratic North Stand scoreboard. City's first foray into the world of high-tech, it gradually deteriorated over the years with numerous bulbs failing before it was finally switched off for the last time in the mid-1980s.

RIGHT: The scoreboard might not have worked, but most other things did during John Bond's relatively brief reign as City manager. Here, Dave Bennett toe pokes home against Crystal Palace in 1981

I am Legend

RIGHT: All hail the messiah, Trevor Francis – arguably City's first superstar signing. Such was the hysteria when he joined from Nottingham Forest, more than 12,000 City fans travelled to Stoke where the new No. 9 announced his arrival by scoring twice in a 3-1 win.

Dismal Days Ahead

Though the 1981/2 campaign began promisingly – by Christmas the Blues topped the table – a disappointing second half of the campaign saw City finish 10th. Pictured here is youth-team product Ray Ranson, one of several local lads to graduate through the ranks.

Bond's second campaign in the hot seat looked for a time as if it may be even more exciting than the first, especially when England striker Trevor Francis was signed from Nottingham Forest. Four weeks later and – just as Dennis Tueart had done 18 months earlier – another former hero re-signed for the Blues. Asa Hartford, one of the big-name casualties of Malcolm Allison's purge, had never wanted to leave City in the first place and the midfielder was happy to return. The manager then signed his son Kevin from Seattle Sounders to bolster the defence. By Christmas the Blues were challenging at the top of the table and a fantastic display at Anfield on Boxing Day gave Bond's men a 3-1 win – their first victory there for almost three decades. Two days later and the Blues went top with a 2-1 over Wolves, but they could not maintain their challenge and like a horse that shows too early in a race, they fell away dramatically with just five more wins from the final 22 games.

Bond's magic seemed to be fading as was his infectious enthusiasm. Trevor Francis was sold to Sampdoria and only Bobby McDonald remained from the famed tartan trio. The in-coming players were, in general, an odd assortment of bargain-basement journeymen and lower League unknowns. The writing was on the wall for all to see and a 4-0 thrashing in the FA Cup fourth round at Brighton was the final straw for Bond who resigned.

RIGHT: Alex Williams makes his debut for City and becomes the first black goalkeeper to play in the Football League.

BELOW: Bobby McDonald deputizes for the injured Joe Corrigan after just three minutes as City cling on to record a 1-0 win over Watford and go to the top of the table.

Down and Out – The Decline Continues

City steadily slipped towards the unthinkable – relegation – with a series of inept displays throughout the 1982/3 campaign. With John Bond gone and Joe Corrigan allowed to leave (mainly to save on his wages), the Blues were a rudderless ship under the stewardship of Bond's former assistant, John Benson, in his first managerial role. What a time to take gambles. City sunk like a stone under Benson's leadership and were left with a dramatic scenario on the final day. Needing only a point to stay up, City couldn't even manage that, conceding a late goal to Raddy Antic, and were relegated. As fans fought with Luton players, it seemed the FA might punish the Blues by forcing them to play several games behind closed doors, though ultimately demotion to the second tier was deemed punishment enough.

Cars   Tetley Bittermen. Yo

Luton's Brian Stein takes on an angry mob of supporters on a day to forget for all concerned.

May 1983: Police keep crowds under control outside the stadium as fans demand the resignation of chairman Peter Swales.

Ugly scenes as the City fans invade the pitch following Luton Town's smash-and-grab relegation decider in May 1983.